# Preserving
# Public Tr...st

---

## The Five Principles of
## Public Service Ethics

By

Michael Josephson and
the Government Ethics
Center Commission of the
Josephson Institute of Ethics

---

A production of the Department of Publications and
Communications at the Josephson Institute of Ethics

| Wes Hanson | | Steve Nish | |
| VP/ Department Director | | Senior Editor / Webmaster | |

| Dan McNeill | Melissa Mertz | Andrew Acalinovich | Peter Chen |
| Editor | Instructional Designer | Art Director | Assistant Editor / Graphics |

---

Unlimited Publishing
Bloomington, Indiana

Josephson Institute of Ethics
Los Angeles, California

Commission members of the Government Ethics Center at the Josephson Institute of Ethics drafted this resource's principles, standards and guidelines in 1990. These commissioners expressed only their own views in this exercise, not necessarily those of the organizations they represented.

The Josephson Institute has updated this edition of *Preserving the Public Trust: the Five Principles of Public Service Ethics* with a new introduction and current (2002) excerpts from the Office of Government Ethics' rules for federal employees.

# Preserving the Public Trust

## The Five Principles of Public Service Ethics

### TABLE OF CONTENTS

# INTRODUCTION

Difficult constituencies. Corrosive cynicism. Obstructive partisanship. Crippling regulations. Scandal-mongering media. Damaging investigations. Huge penalties.

No doubt about it: managing public institutions has never been tougher.

It's crucial to fulfill legal requirements, but a mere compliance mentality can promote a false sense of security, putting you at even greater risk. That's because "wrongdoing" is an ethical concept even more than a legal one. Accusations alone can harm reputations, drain morale, hamper the ability to attract top talent, and divert attention from the efficient delivery of public service.

The most practical strategy is to develop a culture where **_principles of public service_** animate all decision making. This book explores five such principles, as developed by commissioners at the Government and Ethics Center at the Josephson Institute of Ethics.

Leadership training in ethics is also basic to sustaining a successful organization. The Institute offers the nation's premier seminars to help public service leaders transform workplace cultures and achieve sustainable success. There are specialized programs for city/county managers, law enforcement (POST certified plan 4 in California), and school administrators.

The nonprofit, nonpartisan Institute is the nation's leader in ethics training because it focuses on what works in the real world. Its public service programs address a spectrum of issues, from conflicts of interest to dealing with the media to evaluating character in hiring and promoting employees.

The Institute's unique approach also stresses the value of collaboration. Its numerous services for a wide range of community institutions — public, educational, nonprofit, human-service and corporate — reinforce individual ethics initiatives. Other Institute projects include: CHARACTER COUNTS!, the nation's most widely implemented approach to character education; the Pursuing Victory With Honor sportsmanship campaign, endorsed by nearly every major American amateur athletic group; and Ethics and Effectiveness consulting services and programs for corporate officers and directors. All projects offer training programs and support materials.

Michael Josephson is the designer of these initiatives, as well as the lead member of the commission that first drafted this volume. Mr. Josephson is a former law professor and entrepreneur who has become one of the nation's preeminent consultants to federal, state, and local government agencies, including the U.S. Army, the Internal Revenue Service, the FBI, and dozens of city and county government associations and local law enforcement departments. His award-winning daily radio commentaries air nationwide, as well as overseas. He has received the America's Award for Integrity presented by former president Ronald Reagan, and he served as a nonpartisan expert on education for the Bush-Cheney Transition Team.

To help individuals improve, the Institute seeks to:
• Stimulate moral ambition.
• Heighten the ability to perceive the ethical dimension of choices.
• Teach how to discern the most effective ethical responses.
• Show how to implement these responses intelligently.

The Institute enhances organizational ethics by helping leaders to:
• Identify the ethical obligations arising from positions of authority.
• Consider the impact of all institutional actions on all stakeholders.
• Create workplaces that reward ethical and discourage unethical conduct.

The Institute's services include:
• Presentations and keynote addresses
• Workshops, seminars and community forums
• Customized on-site training
• Ethics audits and consulting, including services related to standards/codes of conduct
• Media commentary
• Ethics and Effectiveness in the Workplace seminars
• Character Development Seminars
• *Pursuing Victory With Honor* sportsmanship seminars
• *Honor Above All* academic integrity materials
• *Foundations for Life* quotation-based essay contest
• Publications, videos and communications

For more information:
**Josephson Institute of Ethics**
9841 Airport Blvd., #300, Los Angeles, CA 90045
(310) 846-4800 • (800) 711-2670
**www.josephsoninstitute.org**
**www.charactercounts.org**

# OVERVIEW

The essential ethical qualities of *trustworthiness*, *respect*, *responsibility*, *fairness*, *caring* and *good citizenship* apply to everyone in society. The Josephson Institute calls these the Six Pillars of Character. The Institute also advocates five principles as especially relevant to public sector employees.

In this volume, we have broken down each of these principles into standards followed by guidelines and discussion. In addition, excerpts of rules established by the Office of Government Ethics (OGE) are included as they relate to each principle. (Selections from the OGE rules are extracted from the 2002 update of federal ethics laws, executive orders and regulations.)

---

## THE FIVE PRINCIPLES OF PUBLIC SERVICE

### PRINCIPLE 1:
### *Safeguard the Public Interest*
Public office is a trust; use it only to advance public interests, not personal gain.

### PRINCIPLE 2:
### *Use Independent, Objective Judgment*
Make decisions on the merits, free from partiality, prejudice or conflicts of interest.

### PRINCIPLE 3:
### *Be Publicly Accountable*
Conduct government openly, efficiently, equitably and honorably so the public can make informed judgments and hold public officials accountable.

### PRINCIPLE 4:
### *Lead With Citizenship*
Honor and respect democratic principles. Observe the letter and spirit of laws.

### PRINCIPLE 5:
### *Show Respectability and Fitness for Office*
Safeguard public confidence in the integrity of government by avoiding appearances of impropriety and unbefitting conduct.

---

# EXECUTIVE ORDER 12674

## Principles of Ethical Conduct for Government Officers and Employees

a) Public service is a public trust, requiring employees to place loyalty to the Constitution, the laws, and ethical principles above private gain.

b) Employees shall not hold financial interests that conflict with the conscientious performance of duty.

c) Employees shall not engage in financial transactions using non-public Government information or allow the improper use of such information to further any private interest.

d) An employee shall not, except pursuant to such reasonable exceptions as are provided by regulation, solicit or accept any gift or other item of monetary value from any person or entity seeking official action from doing business with, or conducting activities regulated by the employee's agency, or whose interests may be substantially affected by the performance or nonperformance of the employee's duties.

e) Employees shall put forth honest effort in the performance of their duties.

f) Employees shall make no unauthorized commitments or promises of any kind purporting to bind the Government.

g) Employees shall not use public office for private gain.

h) Employees shall act impartially and not give preferential treatment to any private organization or individual.

i) Employees shall protect and conserve Federal property and shall not use it for other than authorized activities.

j) Employees shall not engage in outside employment or activities, including seeking or negotiating for employment, that conflict with official Government duties and responsibilities.

k) Employees shall disclose waste, fraud, abuse, and corruption to appropriate authorities.

l) Employees shall satisfy in good faith their obligations as citizens, including all just financial obligations, especially those - such as Federal, State, or local taxes - that are imposed by law.

m) Employees shall adhere to all laws and regulations that provide equal opportunity for all Americans regardless of race, color, religion, sex, national origin, age, or handicap.

n) Employees shall endeavor to avoid any actions creating the appearance that they are violating the law or the ethical standards promulgated pursuant to this order.

# PRINCIPLE 1:
## Safeguard the Public Interest

Public employees should treat their office as a public trust, only using the powers and resources of public office to advance public interests, and not to attain personal benefits or pursue any other private interest incompatible with the public good.

Pursuit of the public interest establishes one of the most fundamental principles of public service ethics. An fundamental principle of government ethics is that public office is a public trust. Public servants are obligated to administer their trust solely for the benefit of the public and they should not permit the use of their office for the benefit of any private interest.

The following standards will be discussed in this section:

### I. IMPLEMENTING POLICY

#### A. Who is Responsible for Formulating Policy?

#### B. Subordination of Personal Views

#### C. Dealing with Policy Disagreements

### II. PERSONAL GAIN FROM:

#### A. Public Duties

#### B. Use of Employees

#### C. Use of Government Property

#### D. Use of Title

### III. ISSUES OF LOYALTY

# I
# IMPLEMENTING POLICY

*STANDARD*

Public administrators and executives should interpret and implement policies and laws in good faith and energetically pursue the goals of policy and lawmakers.

The effectiveness of laws and policies is determined not only by what administrators do, but how they do it. Agency officials, bureaucrats, and live officers can determine the efficacy of legislation by the way they allocate resources and carry out their duties. Three issues related to implementing policy are:

> A. *Who Is Responsible for Making Policy?*
>
> B. *Subordination of Personal Views*
>
> C. *Dealing With Policy Disagreements*

## I(A)
## Who is Responsible for Formulating Policy?

*STANDARD*

Persons with the responsibility for making public policy and laws should place the public interest over all other considerations. In a democracy, public interest should be determined and translated into policies and programs by or under the direction of elected officials who are ultimately accountable to the public.

**GUIDELINES AND COMMENTARY**

While rule-making is often delegated to policy-makers and public employees, it is important to remember that elected officials are directly accountable for policy and programs.

# I(B)
# Subordination of Personal Views

### STANDARD

Public employees charged with the administration of policies and laws should do so as equitably, efficiently, and economically as possible, regardless of their personal views. Six issues associated with the subordination of personal views are:

1. *Practical Power*
2. *Tension Between Legislative and Executive Branches*
3. *Separation of Powers*
4. *Dealing With Ambiguity*
5. *Role of Personal Convictions*
6. *Administrators Should Defer to Legislators*

### GUIDELINES AND COMMENTARY

### 1. *Practical Power*

Because of the law's ambiguity and sometimes inconsistent language, public administrators have wide discretion. Such power should be used carefully, openly, and with a "good faith" attempt to honor the will of the formal policy-makers.

### 2. *Tension Between Legislative and Executive Branches*

In some cases, the exercise by public administrators of the practical power to nullify or modify a policy through administrative strategies can be most frustrating to legislators who feel helpless in the face of an all-powerful, unresponsive bureaucracy. At the same time, career executives can be equally frustrated by the passage of laws which have not sufficiently drawn on the expertise of administrators and are thus, impractical, underfunded or ineffective. This common tension between the executive and legislative branches should be eased by closer collaboration and more open communication.

### 3. *Separation of Powers*

In a democracy, policy disagreements should be resolved by democratic processes consistent with the separation of powers between the legislative and executive branches of government. Thus, it is improper for public employees to nullify legislators and senior executive policy makers to impose their own views of the public interest.

## 4. *Dealing with Ambiguity*

It is especially difficult, but no less critical, for public administrators to implement policies with energy and commitment when the intent or goals of a law are unclear or the legislative language is ambiguous. Ambiguity is so prevalent that it is important that it not be used as an excuse to avoid complex, arduous, or ideologically offensive tasks. The fundamental duty of government executives is to act. Refusing to do so invariably obstructs the purposes of policy-makers and denies the intended benefits of a new law or policy. In many cases, the ambiguities can be resolved with reasonable confidence simply by examining the legislative history and the legislation as a whole. In others, further clarification must be sought by whatever mechanisms are available.

## 5. *Role of Personal Convictions*

Government employees, at all levels, usually have personal convictions affecting their interpretation and implementation of policies. This is proper so long as their values and attitudes do not impede or nullify the will of law and policy-makers.

## 6. *Administrators Showing Deference to Legislators*

As a result of superior information and specialized expertise, those who implement policies and laws often have, and almost always think they have, a greater understanding of the issues than the legislative bodies that formulate policies. *Administrators should, of course, seek to bring their information and expertise to bear on the policy-making process by testimony, reports and any other means available.*

Superior knowledge or wisdom, however, does not alter the obligation inherent in representative democracy to defer to lawful processes which invest primary decision making authority with elected officials. Fidelity to democratic principles and our Constitutional form of government makes it improper for administrators to undermine or nullify the will of the legislature in pursuit of their own views of public interest.

# I(C)
# Dealing With Policy Disagreements

*STANDARD*

Public employees who find that their personal convictions are irreconcilably incompatible with lawful policies should openly state their conflict and, in some cases, withdraw from the administration of such policies.

In dealing with policy disagreements, there is a need to address:

1. *Professional Duty vs. Personal Conscience*
2. *Internal Conflicts of Interest*

*GUIDELINES AND COMMENTARY*

## 1. *Professional Duty vs. Personal Conscience*

Ethical government cannot exist without people of principle and conscience. Sometimes, personal convictions of public administrators sharply conflict with the legitimately established policies set by others, so much so that they raise issues of personal integrity. Conflicts most commonly arise when major changes in direction are dictated by a new law or policy. Often such changes are personally and professionally distasteful to public employees committed to existing programs and former policies. Strong beliefs that a new policy is irrational, impractical, unduly political or ideological offensive present a serious ethical dilemma — professional duty versus conscience.

## 2. *Internal Conflicts of Interest*

The existence of strong disagreements with lawful policies by those assigned to interpret or implement them may create unacceptable conflicts of interest between the dictates of conscience and the requirements of law and public service. The public is entitled to vigorous good faith implementation of policies and laws established by or under the direction of its elected representatives. Thus, those who have strong personal beliefs about the government's proper role and the value of specific programs must decide among the following options:

      i) to subordinate their personal views and do their duty;

      ii) to confront the issue directly and refuse to perform; or

      iii) in extreme cases, to resign or request a transfer.

If government is to work, however, the professional obligation to do one's job should prevail most of the time. *It is therefore, ethically proper for conscience-driven public employees to subordinate even the most strongly held personal views and abide by organizational policies so long as they believe they can do so effectively.* At the same time, where they find the duties of office irreconcilable with the dictates of conscience, it is also proper that they remove themselves from the dilemma by resigning or seeking a transfer. *It is not proper, however, to covertly seek to sabotage or hinder government policies.*

# II(A)
# Personal Gain From Performance
# of Public Duties

*STANDARD*

Except for official compensation, public employees should neither seek nor accept any form of payment, gratuity or other personal benefit relating to the performance of their responsibilities.

---

**OGE RULES:**

**Section 2635.702(a) Inducement or coercion of benefits.** An employee shall not use or permit the use of his Government position or title or any authority associated with his public office in a manner that is intended to coerce or induce another person, including a subordinate, to provide any benefit, financial or otherwise, to himself or to friends, relatives, or persons with whom the employee is affiliated in a nongovernmental capacity.

Example 1: Offering to pursue a relative's consumer complaint over a household appliance, an employee of the Securities and Exchange Commission called the general counsel of the manufacturer and, in the course of discussing the problem,

---

stated that he worked at the SEC and was responsible for reviewing the company's filings. The employee violated the prohibition against use of public office for private gain by invoking his official authority in an attempt to influence action to benefit his relative.

Example 2: An employee of the Department of Commerce was asked by a friend to determine why his firm's export license had not yet been granted by another office within the Department of Commerce. At a department-level staff meeting, the employee raised as a matter for official inquiry the delay in approval of the particular license and asked that the particular license be expedited. The official used her public office in an attempt to benefit her friend and, in acting as her friend's agent for the purpose of pursuing the export license with the Department of Commerce, may also have violated 18 U.S.C. 205.

Two issues that are related to personal gain from public duties are:

## 1. *The Impropriety of Personal Benefits*

### STANDARD

Public employees should neither seek nor accept any form of personal benefit for the performance of their duty to deal with a matter promptly, efficiently or fairly or for the exercise of appropriate but discretionary representational authority.

## 2. *The Appearance of the Need for Personal Benefit*

### STANDARD

Public employees should not engage in any conduct which could create in the mind of a reasonable observer the belief that persons will receive better or different service if they provide personal benefits or political support to a government official.

### GUIDELINES AND COMMENTARY

### *What Is the Impropriety of Having Personal Benefits?*

Public employees have an obligation to perform their duties promptly, efficiently and fairly. In addition, some have oversight and representational duties which involve inquiry and intervention on behalf of constituents. Even if the benefit has no affect on the decisions or actions of the public servant, it is improper to seek or accept unofficial compensation or benefits of any sort for the performance of a public duty. While the issue of accepting gifts is certainly an issue of public trust, it is also a problem which affects the independence and objectivity of public employees, and therefore is discussed in that section. (For OGE rules on gifts, please see Principle 2(I)(D) of the this manual.)

The essence of this principle is that *public office should only be used to advance public interests and not to attain personal benefits*. It is related to but different than Principle II, which mandates the exercise of independent objective judgement and forbids conflicts of interest which tend to impede such judgement. Thus, it is no defense to a charge that public office was used for private gain that the public servant in fact did exercise independent judgement and that official actions were in no way influenced by the benefit conferred or sought. It is not even a defense that, under the circumstances, the benefit did not create the appearance of undue influence. It is enough that the personal gain was sought or received.

## II(B)
## Use of an Employee's Own Time
## for Personal Gain

### STANDARD
Public employees should not use other public employees, government time, for private benefit. Likewise, public employees should refuse to perform improper personal tasks on government time.

---

**OGE RULES:**

**Section 2635.705 Use of official time.**

(a) **Use of an employee's own time**. Unless authorized in accordance with law or regulations to use such time for other purposes, an employee shall use official time in an honest

---

effort to perform official duties. An employee not under a leave system, including a Presidential appointee exempted under 5 U.S.C. 6301(2), has an obligation to expend an honest effort and a reasonable proportion of his time in the performance of official duties.

Example 1: An employee of the Social Security Administration may use official time to engage in certain representational activities on behalf of the employee union of which she is a member. Under 5 U.S.C. 7131, this is a proper use of her official time even though it does not involve performance of her assigned duties as a disability claims examiner.

Example 2: A pharmacist employed by the Department of Veterans Affairs has been granted excused absence to participate as a speaker in a conference on drug abuse sponsored by the professional association to which he belongs. Although excused absence granted by an agency in accordance with guidance in chapter 630 of the Federal Personnel Manual allows an employee to be absent from his official duties without charge to his annual leave account, such absence is not on official time.

(b) **Use of a subordinate's time**. An employee shall not encourage, direct, coerce, or request a subordinate to use official time to perform activities other than those required in the performance of official duties or authorized in accordance with law or regulation.

Example 1: An employee of the Department of Housing and Urban Development may not ask his secretary to type his personal correspondence during duty hours. Further, directing or coercing a subordinate to perform such activities during nonduty hours constitutes an improper use of public office for private gain in violation of § 2635.702(a). Where the arrangement is entirely voluntary and appropriate compensation is paid, the secretary may type the correspondence at home on her own time. Where the compensation is not adequate, however, the arrangement would involve a gift to the superior in violation of the standards in subpart C of this part.

A public employee's time is public property which should not be misappropriated to personal use. The following issues are relevant to this point:

1. *The Need for Flexibility*
2. *The Respect for Employee's Own Time*
3. *The Subordinate's Responsibility to Refuse to Do Personal Tasks for Superiors*

**GUIDELINES AND COMMENTARY**

### 1. Why the Need for Flexibility in Relying on Staff for Assisting Personal Needs?

A public executive should be permitted to make moderate use of staff to help organize and schedule the executive's calendar, including some events of a private nature. Emphasis, however, must be placed on the word "moderate" and both the aide and the official must be vigilant to avoid actual abuse as well as the creation of the appearance of unreasonable use of public personnel.

Though this limitation should be interpreted in a reasonable manner given the responsibility of the public official, purely personal errands such as dropping off laundry, picking up children, and purchasing private gifts are justifiable only in extraordinary circumstances where the task is suddenly necessary to help the public executive perform professional duties.

### 2. What Does it Mean to Respect an Employee's Own Time?

Generally, employees do not voluntarily contribute their personal time to benefit their employers. Yet public officials sometimes claim that employees willingly perform personal services "on their own time" — during lunch hour, after normal working hours. Such claims should be examined with skepticism as there is a high risk that the employees believed that they were required to perform personal work as part of their jobs; there is at least an appearance of improper exploitation and such use of public personnel should be avoided.

### 3. *What is the Subordinate's Responsibility in Doing Personal Tasks for a Superior?*

While it is improper for a superior to ask a subordinate to perform personal services, it is also improper for a subordinate, as a public servant, to accede to such requests. While tact is imperative as a practical matter, employees still have the obligation to assure that their services are not converted to nongovernmental uses. *It is improper for the supervisor to harass, pressure, embarrass, intimidate, or punish an employee who properly refuses to perform personal services.*

# II(C)
# Use of Government Property
# for Personal Benefit

*STANDARD*

A public employee should not use government proper facilities for private benefit. Public facilities, equipment and services (office space, typewriters, word processors, telephones, postage, stationery, mailing facilities, photocopying, etc.) should not be appropriated for personal benefit.

---

**OGE RULES:**

**Section 2635.101(b)(9)**

Employees shall protect and conserve Federal property and shall not use it for other than authorized activities.

**Section 2635.702(a) Use of public office for private gain.**

An employee shall not use his public office for his own private gain, for the endorsement of any product, service or enterprise, or for the private gain of friends, relatives, or persons with whom the employee is affiliated in a nongovernmental capacity, including nonprofit organizations of which the employee is an officer or member, and persons with whom the employee has or seeks employment or business relations. The specific prohibitions set forth in paragraphs (a) through (d) of this section apply this general standard, but are not

---

intended to be exclusive or to limit the application of this section.

(a) **Inducement or coercion of benefits**. An employee shall not use or permit the use of his Government position or title or any authority associated with his public office in a manner that is intended to coerce or induce another person, including a subordinate, to provide any benefit, financial or otherwise, to himself or to friends, relatives, or persons with whom the employee is affiliated in a nongovernmental capacity.

Example 1: Offering to pursue a relative's consumer complaint over a household appliance, an employee of the Securities and Exchange Commission called the general counsel of the manufacturer and, in the course of discussing the problem, stated that he worked at the SEC and was responsible for reviewing the company's filings. The employee violated the prohibition against use of public office for private gain by invoking his official authority in an attempt to influence action to benefit his relative.

Example 2: An employee of the Department of Commerce was asked by a friend to determine why his firm's export license had not yet been granted by another office within the Department of Commerce. At a department-level staff meeting, the employee raised as a matter for official inquiry the delay in approval of the particular license and asked that the particular license be expedited. The official used her public office in an attempt to benefit her friend and, in acting as her friend's agent for the purpose of pursuing the export license with the Department of Commerce, may also have violated 18 U.S.C. 205.

**Section 2635.703 Use of nonpublic information**.

(a) **Prohibition**. An employee shall not engage in a financial transaction using nonpublic information, nor allow the improper use of nonpublic information to further his own private interest or that of another, whether through advice or recommendation, or by knowing unauthorized disclosure.

(b) **Definition of nonpublic information**. For purposes of this section, nonpublic information is information that the employee gains by reason of Federal employment and that he knows or reasonably should know has not been made available to the general public. It includes information that he knows or reasonably should know:

(1) Is routinely exempt from disclosure under 5 U.S.C. 552 or otherwise protected from disclosure by statute, Executive order or regulation;

(2) Is designated as confidential by an agency; or

(3) Has not actually been disseminated to the general public and is not authorized to be made available to the public on request.

Example 1: A Navy employee learns in the course of her duties that a small corporation will be awarded a Navy contract for electrical test equipment. She may not take any action to purchase stock in the corporation or its suppliers and she may not advise friends or relatives to do so until after public announcement of the award. Such actions could violate Federal securities statutes as well as this section.

Example 2: A General Services Administration employee involved in evaluating proposals for a construction contract cannot disclose the terms of a competing proposal to a friend employed by a company bidding on the work. Prior to award of the contract, bid or proposal information is nonpublic information specifically protected by 41 U.S.C. 423.

Example 3: An employee is a member of a source selection team assigned to review the proposals submitted by several companies in response to an Army solicitation for spare parts. As a member of the evaluation team, the employee has access to proprietary information regarding the production methods of Alpha Corporation, one of the competitors. He may not use that information to assist Beta Company in drafting a proposal to compete for a Navy spare parts contract. The Federal Acquisition Regulation in 48 CFR parts 3, 14 and 15 restricts the release of information related to procurements and other contractor information that must be protected under 18 U.S.C. 1905 and 41 U.S.C. 423.

Example 4: An employee of the Nuclear Regulatory Commission inadvertently includes a document that is exempt from disclosure with a group of documents released in response to a Freedom of Information Act request. Regardless of whether the document is used improperly, the employee's disclosure does not violate this section because it was not a knowing unauthorized disclosure made for the purpose of furthering a private interest.

Example 5: An employee of the Army Corps of Engineers is actively involved in the activities of an organization whose goals relate to protection of the environment. The employee may not, other than as permitted by agency procedures, give the organization or a newspaper reporter nonpublic information about long-range plans to build a particular dam.

**Section 2635.704 Use of Government property.**

(a) **Standard**. An employee has a duty to protect and conserve Government property and shall not use such property, or allow its use, for other than authorized purposes.

(b) **Definitions**. For purposes of this section:

(1) Government property includes any form of real or personal property in which the Government has an ownership, leasehold, or other property interest as well as any right or other intangible interest that is purchased with Government funds, including the services of contractor personnel. The term includes office supplies, telephone and other telecommunications equipment and services, the Government mails, automated data processing capabilities, printing and reproduction facilities, Government records, and Government vehicles.

(2) Authorized purposes are those purposes for which Government property is made available to members of the public or those purposes authorized in accordance with law or regulation.

Example 1: Under regulations of the General Services Administration at 41 CFR 101-35.201, an employee may make a personal long distance call charged to her personal calling card.

Example 2: An employee of the Commodity Futures Trading

Commission whose office computer gives him access to a commercial service providing information for investors may not use that service for personal investment research.

Example 3: In accordance with Office of Personnel Management regulations at part 251 of this title, an attorney employed by the Department of Justice may be permitted to use her office word processor and agency photocopy equipment to prepare a paper to be presented at a conference sponsored by a professional association of which she is a member.

# II(D)
# Use of Title for Personal Benefit

*STANDARD*

Public employees should not use, nor allow others to use, the authority, title, or prestige of public office for the attainment of private financial, social or political benefits in any manner that is inconsistent with public interests.

## OGE RULES:

**Section 2635.702(b) Appearance of governmental sanction.**

Except as otherwise provided in this part, an employee shall not use or permit the use of his Government position or title or any authority associated with his public office in a manner that could reasonably be construed to imply that his agency or the Government sanctions or endorses his personal activities or those of another. When teaching, speaking, or writing in a personal capacity, he may refer to his official title or position only as permitted by Section 2635.807(b). He may sign a letter of recommendation using his official title only in response to a request for an employment recommendation or character reference based upon personal knowledge of the ability or character of an individual with whom he has dealt in the course of Federal employment or whom he is recommending for Federal employment.

Example 1: An employee of the Department of the Treasury who is asked to provide a letter of recommendation for a former subordinate on his staff may provide the recommendation using official stationery and may sign the letter using his official title. If, however, the request is for the recommendation of a personal friend with whom he has not dealt in the Government, the employee should not use official stationery or sign the letter of recommendation using his official title, unless the recommendation is for Federal employment. In writing the letter of recommendation for his personal friend, it may be appropriate for the employee to refer to his official position in the body of the letter.

**Section 2635.702(e) Use of terms of address and ranks.**

Nothing in this section prohibits an employee who is ordinarily addressed using a general term of address, such as "The Honorable," or a rank, such as a military or ambassadorial rank, from using that term of address or rank in connection with a personal activity.

Given this standard, the three issues dealing with personal benefits of using titles are:

1. *When Is It Acceptable To Use Official Titles?*
2. *What Precautions Must Be Taken by Those Holding High Public Office?*
3. *What Are the Misuses of Letterhead?*

### GUIDELINES AND COMMENTARY

1. *When Is It Acceptable To Use An Official Name and Title?*

### STANDARD

Public employees should not permit their names or official titles to be used by a nonpublic enterprise in any manner which would lead reasonable observers to believe that those who deal with the enterprise may receive special treatment or advantages as a result of a formal association with the public servant.

In discussing the appropriateness of using names and titles, four common issues that are of concern are:

- *Board Membership and Consulting*
- *Premium Compensation*
- *Normal Compensation*
- *Duty to Reduce the Appearance of Impropriety*

### Board Membership and Consulting

Nonpublic enterprises of all sorts, including nonprofit associations, charitable organizations, corporations and firms involved in lobbying, public relations, law practice and consulting often seek out persons serving in government to serve on boards, advisory committees or as consultants. The most serious problems arise when the public servant is compensated by the enterprise. All such associations raise ethical problems because of the possibility that public office is used by the public employee, the enterprise that retains him or her, or both, for private benefit.

### Premium Compensation

The problem is most acute when, because of the public servant's title and position, the compensation is more than the normal market value of the services rendered. It is especially important because of the public servant's title and position, the compensation is more than the normal market value of the services rendered. It is especially important when public employees receive outside income that the compensation commensurate with the actual personal services rendered. If any premium is being paid due to the public servant's position, or no significant services are being rendered, the enterprise is, in effect, improperly buying, and the public servant is, in effect, improperly selling the prestige associated with the office.

### Normal Compensation

Where the compensation paid for services is proportional to the services performed by normal market standards, or the service is uncompensated, the impropriety is less severe. But even such relationships may improperly use public office. For example, clients or customers may seek representation by a firm employing a public servant because they think that they will have some special advantage in dealing with government as a result of the association with the public employee. Generally, the public servant should avoid associations which create a reasonable possibility that private interests will be significantly enhanced because the employee also holds public office.

### Duty to Reduce Appearance of Impropriety

Public employees who associate with private enterprises have a special duty to assure that these enterprises do not suggest or imply special influence with government and that the clients and customers of the enterprise are not led to expect or encouraged to think that the fact that public officials work with them or have lent their names to the enterprise will provide any economic advantage.

### 2. What Precautions Must Be Taken by Those Holding High Public Office?

#### STANDARD

The present or former holder of a high public office which carries with it substantial prestige should not appear to sell the stature of the office by accepting sums that create a general perception that the office has been exploited for private gain.

There is a concern particularly with *cashing in* and *considering all the circumstances*.

### Cashing In

Regardless of legality, it is unseemly when present or former government officials appear to blatantly be "cashing in" on their government service by acting as consultants, lobbyists, board members or spokespersons for private interests in circumstances where it appears that they are peddling influence or selling the prestige and stature of their prior office.

*Considering All the Circumstances*

The problem becomes especially serious when former public employees are paid a premium — an amount above the normal market value for the services rendered — because of their political connections or the inherent prestige they bring to a private enterprise. This is not to say that former government officials who have important experiences cannot serve on boards, make speeches for substantial fees or engage in consulting or lobbying. The circumstances including how, when and at what price they sell their services are of critical importance. If political connections are used, or unduly influence former colleagues or subordinates, it is improper. If the services of a present or former government official are used in close proximity to actions taken by the official or he  or she receives significant gift or benefits shortly after leaving government service, it is likely to be improper. And, if the fee paid for a few phone calls or meetings or for appearances are in no way commensurate with the work performed or the normal fee for similar services, it is improper.

## 3. *What Are the Misuses of Letterhead?*

### STANDARD
Public employees should not use official letterhead or refer to their public position as a means of inducing or intimidating persons to resolve disputes more favorably, provide preferential treatment, favors or other advantages.

There are several reasons why official name dropping to obtain special treatment is improper. First, those who give favors to public employees because of their positions often expect favors in return. In such cases, the transaction too closely resembles bribery — favor to favor. Second, some persons who accede to requests for preferential treatment or favors to public employees do so out of fear that if they do not, the official may seek reprisal. In those cases, the transaction looks too much like extortion.

# III
# ISSUES OF LOYALTY

*STANDARD*

Loyalty is an issue that is of great concern when dealing with policy issues because it can bias the outcome of policy and policies.

In formulating public policy, the issues of loyalty are:

1. *Competing Loyalties*
2. *Ranking Loyalty*
3. *Organizational vs. Personal Loyalty*

As discussed previously, public interest should be the criteria basis for people making public policy and laws. In a democracy, public interest should be determined and translated into policies and programs by or under the direction of elected officials who are ultimately accountable to the public.

*GUIDELINES AND COMMENTARY*

1. *What Are Competing Loyalties?*

*STANDARD*

In pursuing the public interest, public employees should put loyalty to democratic principles and to the broadest public good above loyalty to political parties, constituencies and individuals.

Napoleon reportedly pointed out that there are two types of loyalty: *dog loyalty* and *cat loyalty*. Cat loyalty incorporates the notion of the "greatest good for the greatest number." The public employee is seen to be more loyal to the "house" rather than to the "master." While decisions need to be based on a case-by-case basis, the principle of public service generally requires public employees to pursue the greatest long term good over the largest amount of people. It also implies that broader interests over smaller, narrower ones: country over state, state over community, community over individuals, and principle over party.

Dog loyalty, in contrast, concerns loyalty to the master, the dog's primary interest. Public servants are often held to a number of competing loyalty obligations — to country, state, community, constituency groups, political supporters, government departments, colleagues, supervisors, subordinates, family and self.

## 1. *How Do You Solve Loyalty Conflicts?*

In many political situations, these loyalties conflict. What is best for the country or state may not be good for a particular community; what is good for an individual constituent may not be in the best interest of other constituents or interest groups; and the highest public interest may conflict with personal career ambitions. In order to address this issue of competing loyalties, a priority list needs to be established ranking loyalty obligations.

## 2. *When Do You Rank Loyalty Obligations?*

### STANDARD
In dealing with public funds and general public policies, elected officials and other policy makers need to objectively evaluate information and decide what are the best alternatives for the public as a whole, rather than a narrow constituency.

## 3. *What If the Conflict is Organizational vs. Personal Loyalties?*

### STANDARD
Public employees with supervisory authority should safeguard and protect the public interest, the reputation of government and the integrity and efficiency of their department, even at the cost of injuring a superior, colleague, or friend.

Conflicting loyalty arises where the interests of an organization are inconsistent with those of individuals within the organization. The problem gets even more complicated when loyalty to a particular person within the organization conflicts with loyalty obligations to others.

### *How Can You Minimize Loyalty Conflicts?*

Loyalty conflicts can be minimized by clarifying loyalty expectations as they relate to each individual. Discuss conflicts between personal and organizational needs (e.g., what should a supervisor do if an employee who is supporting a terminally ill relative has an alcohol problem that is affecting his work?) The responsibility of office generally demands placing institutional interests above individual loyalties.

# PRINCIPLE 2:
# Use Independent,
# Objective Judgement

Public employees should employ independent objective judgment in performing their duties, deciding all matters on the merits, free from conflicts of interest and both real and apparent improper influences.

The following standards will be discussed in this section:

## I. CONFLICTS OF INTEREST

### A. Disclosure of Financial Conflicts of Interest

### B. Benefits Intended to Influence (e.g., Gratuities and Gifts)

### C. Duty to Report Improper Offers (i.e., Bribes)

### D. Appearance of Undue Influence

## II. RECUSAL AND DISQUALIFICATIONS

## III. BIAS AND FAVORITISM

## IV. INTERVENING IN ADMINISTRATIVE ACTIONS

---

**OGE RULES:**

**Section 2635.101(b)(2)** Employees shall not hold financial interests that conflict with the conscientious performance of duty.

**Section 2635.101(b)(10)** Employees shall not engage in outside employment or activities, including seeking or negotiating for employment, that conflict with official Government duties and responsibilities.

**Section 2635.801(b)** An employee who wishes to engage in outside employment or other outside activities must comply with all relevant provisions of this subpart, including, when applicable:

---

(1) The prohibition on outside employment or any other outside activity that conflicts with the employee's official duties;

(2) Any agency-specific requirement for prior approval of outside employment or activities;

(3) The limitations on receipt of outside earned income by certain Presidential appointees and other noncareer employees;

(4) The limitations on paid and unpaid service as an expert witness;

(5) The limitations on participation in professional organizations;

(6) The limitations on paid and unpaid teaching, speaking, and writing; and

(7) The limitations on fundraising activities.

(c) Outside employment and other outside activities of an employee must also comply with applicable provisions set forth in other subparts of this part and in supplemental agency regulations. These include the principle that an employee shall endeavor to avoid actions creating an appearance of violating any of the ethical standards in this part and the prohibition against use of official position for an employee's private gain or for the private gain of any person with whom he has employment or business relations or is otherwise affiliated in a nongovernmental capacity.

(d) In addition to the provisions of this and other subparts of this part, an employee who wishes to engage in outside employment or other outside activities must comply with applicable statutes and regulations. Relevant provisions of law, many of which are listed in subpart I of this part, may include:

(1) 18 U.S.C. 201(b), which prohibits a public official from seeking, accepting or agreeing to receive or accept anything of value in return for being influenced in the performance of an official act or for being induced to take or omit to take

any action in violation of his official duty;

(2) 18 U.S.C. 201(c), which prohibits a public official, otherwise than as provided by law for the proper discharge of official duty, from seeking, accepting, or agreeing to receive or accept anything of value for or because of any official act;

(3) 18 U.S.C. 203(a), which prohibits an employee from seeking, accepting, or agreeing to receive or accept compensation for any representational services, rendered personally or by another, in relation to any particular matter in which the United States is a party or has a direct and substantial interest, before any department, agency, or other specified entity. This statute contains several exceptions, as well as standards for special Government employees that limit the scope of the restriction;

(4) 18 U.S.C. 205, which prohibits an employee, whether or not for compensation, from acting as agent or attorney for anyone in a claim against the United States or from acting as agent or attorney for anyone, before any department, agency, or other specified entity, in any particular matter in which the United States is a party or has a direct and substantial interest. It also prohibits receipt of any gratuity, or any share of or interest in a claim against the United States, in consideration for assisting in the prosecution of such claim. This statute contains several exceptions, as well as standards for special Government employees that limit the scope of the restrictions;

(5) 18 U.S.C. 209, which prohibits an employee, other than a special Government employee, from receiving any salary or any contribution to or supplementation of salary from any source other than the United States as compensation for services as a Government employee. The statute contains several exceptions that limit its applicability;

(6) The Emoluments Clause of the United States Constitution, article I, section 9, clause 8, which prohibits anyone holding an office of profit or trust under the United States from accepting any gift, office, title or emolument, including salary or compensation, from any foreign government except as

authorized by Congress. In addition, 18 U.S.C. 219 generally prohibits any public official from being or acting as an agent of a foreign principal, including a foreign government, corporation or person, if the employee would be required to register as a foreign agent under 22 U.S.C. 611 et seq.;

(7) The Hatch Act Reform Amendments, 5 U.S.C. 7321 through 7326, which govern the political activities of executive branch employees; and

(8) The limitations on outside employment, 5 U.S.C. App. (Ethics in Government Act of 1978), which prohibit a covered noncareer employee's receipt of compensation for specified activities and provide that he shall not allow his name to be used by any firm or other entity which provides professional services involving a fiduciary relationship. Implementing regulations are contained in Sections 2636.305 through 2636.307 of this chapter.

### Section 2635.802 Conflicting outside employment and activities.

An employee shall not engage in outside employment or any other outside activity that conflicts with his official duties. An activity conflicts with an employee's official duties:

(a) If it is prohibited by statute or by an agency supplemental regulation; or

(b) If, under the standards set forth in Sections 2635.402 and 2635.502, it would require the employee's disqualification from matters so central or critical to the performance of his official duties that the employee's ability to perform the duties of his position would be materially impaired.

Employees are cautioned that even though an outside activity may not be prohibited under this section, it may violate other principles or standards set forth in this part or require the employee to disqualify himself from participation in certain particular matters under either subpart D or subpart E of this part.

Example 1: An employee of the Environmental Protection Agency has just been promoted. His principal duty in his new position is to write regulations relating to the disposal of hazardous waste. The employee may not continue to serve as president of a nonprofit environmental organization that routinely submits comments on such regulations. His service as an officer would require his disqualification from duties critical to the performance of his official duties on a basis so frequent as to materially impair his ability to perform the duties of his position.

Example 2: An employee of the Occupational Safety and Health Administration who was and is expected again to be instrumental in formulating new OSHA safety standards applicable to manufacturers that use chemical solvents has been offered a consulting contract to provide advice to an affected company in restructuring its manufacturing operations to comply with the OSHA standards. The employee should not enter into the consulting arrangement even though he is not currently working on OSHA standards affecting this industry and his consulting contract can be expected to be completed before he again works on such standards. Even though the consulting arrangement would not be a conflicting activity within the meaning of Section 2635.802, it would create an appearance that the employee had used his official position to obtain the compensated outside business opportunity and it would create the further appearance of using his public office for the private gain of the manufacturer.

**Section 2635.803 Prior approval for outside employment and activities.**

When required by agency supplemental regulation issued after February 3, 1993, an employee shall obtain prior approval before engaging in outside employment or activities. Where it is determined to be necessary or desirable for the purpose of administering its ethics program, an agency shall, by supplemental regulation, require employees or any category of employees to obtain prior approval before engaging in specific types of outside activities, including outside employment.

**Section 2635.804 Outside earned income limitations applicable to certain Presidential appointees and other noncareer employees.**

(a) **Presidential appointees to full-time noncareer positions**. A Presidential appointee to a full-time noncareer position shall not receive any outside earned income for outside employment, or for any other outside activity, performed during that Presidential appointment. This limitation does not apply to any outside earned income received for outside employment, or for any other outside activity, carried out in satisfaction of the employee's obligation under a contract entered into prior to April 12, 1989.

(b) **Covered noncareer employees**. Covered noncareer employees, as defined in Section 2636.303(a) of this chapter, may not, in any calendar year, receive outside earned income attributable to that calendar year which exceeds 15 percent of the annual rate of basic pay for level II of the Executive Schedule under 5 U.S.C. 5313, as in effect on January 1 of such calendar year. Employees should consult the regulations implementing this limitation, which are contained in Sections 2636.301 through 2636.304 of this chapter. Note: In addition to the 15 percent limitation on outside earned income, covered noncareer employees are prohibited from receiving any compensation for: practicing a profession which involves a fiduciary relationship; affiliating with or being employed by a firm or other entity which provides professional services involving a fiduciary relationship; serving as an officer or member of the board of any association, corporation or other entity; or teaching without prior approval. Implementing regulations are contained in Sections 2636.305 through 2636.307 of this chapter.

(c) **Definitions**. For purposes of this Section:

(1) Outside earned income has the meaning set forth in Section 2636.303(b) of this chapter, except that Section 2636.303(b)(8) shall not apply.

(2) Presidential appointee to a full-time noncareer position means any employee who is appointed by the President to a full-time position described in 5 U.S.C. 5312 through 5317 or to a position that, by statute or as a matter of practice, is filled by Presidential appointment, other than:

(i) A position filled under the authority of 3 U.S.C. 105 or 3 U.S.C. 107(a) for which the rate of basic pay is less than that for GS-9, step 1 of the General Schedule;

(ii) A position, within a White House operating unit, that is designated as not normally subject to change as a result of a Presidential transition;

(iii) A position within the uniformed services; or

(iv) A position in which a member of the foreign service is serving that does not require advice and consent of the Senate.

Example 1: A career Department of Justice employee who is detailed to a policy-making position in the White House Office that is ordinarily filled by a noncareer employee is not a Presidential appointee to a full-time noncareer position.

Example 2: A Department of Energy employee appointed under Section 213.3301 of this title to a Schedule C position is appointed by the agency and, thus, is not a Presidential appointee to a full-time noncareer position.

**Section 2635.805 Service as an expert witness**.

(a) **Restriction**. An employee shall not serve, other than on behalf of the United States, as an expert witness, with or without compensation, in any proceeding before a court or agency of the United States in which the United States is a party or has a direct and substantial interest, unless the employee's participation is authorized by the agency under paragraph (c) of this section. Except as provided in paragraph (b) of this section, this restriction shall apply to a special Government employee only if he has participated as an employee or special Government employee in the particular proceeding or in the particular matter that is the subject of the proceeding.

(b) **Additional restriction applicable to certain special Government employees**. (1) In addition to the restriction described in paragraph (a) of this section, a special Government employee described in paragraph (b) (2) of this section shall not serve, other than on behalf of the United States, as an expert witness, with or without compensation, in any proceeding before a court or agency of the United States in which his employing agency is a party or has a direct and substantial interest, unless the employee's participation is authorized by the agency under paragraph (c) of this section.

(2) The restriction in paragraph (b)(1) of this section shall apply to a special Government employee who:

(i) Is appointed by the President;

(ii) Serves on a commission established by statute; or

(iii) Has served or is expected to serve for more than 60 days in a period of 365 consecutive days.

(c) **Authorization to serve as an expert witness**. Provided that the employee's testimony will not violate any of the principles or standards set forth in this part, authorization to provide expert witness service otherwise prohibited by paragraphs (a) and (b) of this section may be given by the designated agency ethics official of the agency in which the employee serves when:

(1) After consultation with the agency representing the Government in the proceeding or, if the Government is not a party, with the Department of Justice and the agency with the most direct and substantial interest in the matter, the designated agency ethics official determines that the employee's service as an expert witness is in the interest of the Government; or

(2) The designated agency ethics official determines that the subject matter of the testimony does not relate to the employee's official duties within the meaning of Section 2635.807(a)(2)(i).

(d) **Nothing in this section prohibits an employee from serving as a fact witness when subpoenaed by an appropriate authority**.

**Section 2635.806 Participation in professional associations**. [Reserved]

## Section 2635.807 Teaching, speaking and writing

(a) **Compensation for teaching, speaking or writing**. Except as permitted by paragraph (a)(3) of this section, an employee, including a special Government employee, shall not receive compensation from any source other than the Government for teaching, speaking or writing that relates to the employee's official duties.

(1) **Relationship to other limitations on receipt of compensation**. The compensation prohibition contained in this section is in addition to any other limitation on receipt of compensation set forth in this chapter, including:

(i) The requirement contained in Section 2636.307 of this chapter that covered noncareer employees obtain advance authorization before engaging in teaching for compensation; and

(ii) The prohibitions and limitations in Section 2635.804 and in Section 2636.304 of this chapter on receipt of outside earned income applicable to certain Presidential appointees and to other covered noncareer employees.

(2) **Definitions**. For purposes of this paragraph:

(i) Teaching, speaking or writing relates to the employee's official duties if:

(A) The activity is undertaken as part of the employee's official duties;

(B) The circumstances indicate that the invitation to engage in the activity was extended to the employee primarily because of his official position rather than his expertise on the particular subject matter;

(C) The invitation to engage in the activity or the offer of compensation for the activity was extended to the employee, directly or indirectly, by a person who has interests that may be affected substantially by performance or nonperformance of the employee's official duties;

(D) The information conveyed through the activity draws

substantially on ideas or official data that are nonpublic information as defined in Section 2635.703(b); or

(E) Except as provided in paragraph (a)(2)(i)(E)(4) of this section, the subject of the activity deals in significant part with:

(1) Any matter to which the employee presently is assigned or to which the employee had been assigned during the previous one-year period;

(2) Any ongoing or announced policy, program or operation of the agency; or

(3) In the case of a noncareer employee as defined in Section 2636.303(a) of this chapter, the general subject matter area, industry, or economic sector primarily affected by the programs and operations of his agency.

(4) The restrictions in paragraphs (a)(2)(i)(E)(2) and (3) of this section do not apply to a special Government employee. The restriction in paragraph (a)(2)(i)(E)(1) of this section applies only during the current appointment of a special Government employee; except that if the special Government employee has not served or is not expected to serve for more than 60 days during the first year or any subsequent one- year period of that appointment, the restriction applies only to particular matters involving specific parties in which the special Government employee has participated or is participating personally and substantially.

**Note**: Section 2635.807(a)(2)(i)(E) does not preclude an employee, other than a covered noncareer employee, from receiving compensation for teaching, speaking or writing on a subject within the employee's discipline or inherent area of expertise based on his educational background or experience even though the teaching, speaking or writing deals generally with a subject within the agency's areas of responsibility.

Example 1: The Director of the Division of Enforcement at the Commodity Futures Trading Commission has a keen interest in stamp collecting and has spent years developing his own collection as well as studying the field generally. He is asked by an international society of philatelists to give a series of four lectures on how to assess the value of American stamps. Because the subject does not relate to his official duties, the Director may accept compensation for the lecture series. He could not, however, accept a similar invitation from a commodities broker.

Example 2: A scientist at the National Institutes of Health, whose principal area of Government research is the molecular basis of the development of cancer, could not be compensated for writing a book which focuses specifically on the research she conducts in her position at NIH, and thus, relates to her official duties. However, the scientist could receive compensation for writing or editing a textbook on the treatment of all cancers, provided that the book does not focus on recent research at NIH, but rather conveys scientific knowledge gleaned from the scientific community as a whole. The book might include a chapter, among many other chapters, which discusses the molecular basis of cancer development. Additionally, the book could contain brief discussions of recent developments in cancer treatment, even though some of those developments are derived from NIH research, as long as it is available to the public.

Example 3: On his own time, a National Highway Traffic Safety Administration employee prepared a consumer's guide to purchasing a safe automobile that focuses on automobile crash worthiness statistics gathered and made public by NHTSA. He may not receive royalties or any other form of compensation for the guide. The guide deals in significant part with the programs or operations of NHTSA and, therefore, relates to the employee's official duties. On the other hand, the employee could receive royalties from the sale of a consumer's guide to values in used automobiles even though it contains a brief, incidental discussion of automobile safety standards developed by NHTSA.

Example 4: An employee of the Securities and Exchange Commission may not receive compensation for a book which focuses specifically on the regulation of the securities industry in the United States, since that subject concerns the regulatory programs or operations of the SEC. The employee may, however, write a book about the advantages of investing in various types of securities as long as the book contains only an incidental discussion of any program or operation of the SEC.

Example 5: An employee of the Department of Commerce who works in the Department's employee relations office is an acknowledged expert in the field of Federal employee labor relations, and participates in Department negotiations with employee unions. The employee may receive compensation from a private training institute for a series of lectures which describe the decisions of the Federal Labor Relations Authority concerning unfair labor practices, provided that her lectures do not contain any significant discussion of labor relations cases handled at the Department of Commerce, or the Department's labor relations policies. Federal Labor Relations Authority decisions concerning Federal employee unfair labor practices are not a specific program or operation of the Department of Commerce and thus do not relate to the employee's official duties. However, an employee of the FLRA could not give the same presentations for compensation.

Example 6: A program analyst employed at the Environmental Protection Agency may receive royalties and other compensation for a book about the history of the environmental movement in the United States even though it contains brief references to the creation and responsibilities of the EPA. A covered noncareer employee of the EPA, however, could not receive compensation for writing the same book because it deals with the general subject matter area affected by EPA programs and operations. Neither employee could receive compensation for writing a book that focuses on specific EPA regulations or otherwise on its programs and operations.

Example 7: An attorney in private practice has been given a one year appointment as a special Government employee to serve on an advisory committee convened for the purpose of surveying and recommending modification of procurement regulations that deter small businesses from competing for Government contracts. Because his service under that appointment is not expected to exceed 60 days, the attorney may accept compensation for an article about the anticompetitive effects of certain regulatory certification requirements even though those regulations are being reviewed by the advisory committee. The regulations which are the focus of the advisory committee deliberations are not a particular matter involving specific parties. Because the information is nonpublic, he could not, however, accept compensation for an article which recounts advisory committee deliberations that took place in a meeting closed to the public in order to discuss proprietary information provided by a small business.

Example 8: A biologist who is an expert in marine life is employed for more than 60 days in a year as a special Government employee by the National Science Foundation to assist in developing a program of grants by the Foundation for the study of coral reefs. The biologist may continue to receive compensation for speaking, teaching and writing about marine life generally and coral reefs specifically. However, during the term of her appointment as a special Government employee, she may not receive compensation for an article about the NSF program she is participating in developing. Only the latter would concern a matter to which the special Government employee is assigned.

Example 9: An expert on international banking transactions has been given a one-year appointment as a special Government employee to assist in analyzing evidence in the Government's fraud prosecution of owners of a failed savings and loan association. It is anticipated that she will serve fewer than 60 days under that appointment. Nevertheless, during her appointment, the expert may not accept compensation for an article about the fraud prosecution, even though the article does not reveal nonpublic information. The prosecution is a particular matter that involves specific parties.

(ii) Agency has the meaning set forth in Section 2635.102(a), except that any component of a department designated as a separate agency under Section 2635.203(a) shall be considered a separate agency.

(iii) Compensation includes any form of consideration, remuneration or income, including royalties, given for or in connection with the employee's teaching, speaking or writing activities. Unless accepted under specific statutory authority, such as 31 U.S.C. 1353, 5 U.S.C. 4111 or 7342, or an agency gift acceptance statute, it includes transportation, lodgings and meals, whether provided in kind, by purchase of a ticket, by payment in advance or by reimbursement after the expense has been incurred. It does not include:

(A) Items offered by any source that could be accepted from a prohibited source under subpart B of this part;

(B) Meals or other incidents of attendance such as waiver of attendance fees or course materials furnished as part of the event at which the teaching or speaking takes place;

(C) Copies of books or of publications containing articles, reprints of articles, tapes of speeches, and similar items that provide a record of the teaching, speaking or writing activity; or

(D) In the case of an employee other than a covered noncareer employee as defined in 5 CFR 2636.303(a), travel expenses, consisting of transportation, lodgings or meals, incurred in connection with the teaching, speaking or writing activity. Note to Paragraph (a)(2)(iii): Independent of Section 2635.807(a), other authorities, such as 18 U.S.C. 209, in some circumstances may limit or entirely preclude an employee's acceptance of travel expenses. In addition, employees who file financial disclosure reports should be aware that, subject to applicable thresholds and exclusions, travel and travel reimbursements accepted from sources other than the United States Government must be reported on their financial disclosure reports.

Example 1 to paragraph (a)(2)(iii): A GS 15 employee of the Forest Service has developed and marketed, in her private capacity, a speed reading technique for which popular demand is growing. She is invited to speak about the technique by a representative of an organization that will be substantially affected by a regulation on land management which the employee is in the process of drafting for the Forest Service. The representative offers to pay the employee a $200 speaker's fee and to reimburse all her travel expenses. She may accept the travel reimbursements, but not the speaker's fee. The speaking activity is related to her official duties under Section 2635.807(a)(2)(i)(C) and the fee is prohibited compensation for such speech; travel expenses incurred in connection with the speaking engagement, on the other hand, are not prohibited compensation for a GS 15 employee.

Example 2 to paragraph (a)(2)(iii): Solely because of her recent appointment to a Cabinet-level position, a Government official is invited by the Chief Executive Officer of a major international corporation to attend firm meetings to be held in Aspen for the purpose of addressing senior corporate managers on the importance of recreational activities to a balanced lifestyle. The firm offers to reimburse the official's travel expenses. The official may not accept the offer. The speaking activity is related to official duties under Section 2635.807(a)(2)(i)(B) and, because she is a covered noncareer employee as defined in Section 2636.303(a) of this chapter, the travel expenses are prohibited compensation as to her.

Example 3 to paragraph (a)(2)(iii): A GS 14 attorney at the Federal Trade Commission (FTC) who played a lead role in a recently concluded merger case is invited to speak about the case, in his private capacity, at a conference in New York. The attorney has no public speaking responsibilities on behalf of the FTC apart from the judicial and administrative proceedings to which he is assigned. The sponsors of the conference offer to reimburse the attorney for expenses incurred in connection with his travel to New York. They also offer him, as compensation for his time and effort, a free trip to San Francisco. The attorney may accept the travel expenses to New York, but not the expenses to San Francisco. The lecture relates to his official duties under paragraphs (a)(2)(i)(E)(1) and (a)(2)(i)(E) (2) of Section 2635.807, but because he is not a covered noncareer employee as defined in Section 2636.303(a) of this chapter, the expenses associated with his travel to New York are not a prohibited form of compensation as to him. The travel expenses to San Francisco, on the other hand, not incurred in connection with the speaking activity, are a prohibited form of compensation. If the attorney were a covered noncareer employee he would be barred from accepting the travel expenses to New York as well as the travel expenses to San Francisco.

Example 4 to paragraph (a)(2)(iii): An advocacy group dedicated to improving treatments for severe pain asks the National Institutes of Health (NIH) to provide a conference speaker who can discuss recent advances in the agency's research on pain. The group also offers to pay the employee's travel expenses to attend the conference. After performing the required conflict of interest analysis, NIH authorizes acceptance of the travel expenses under 31 U.S.C. 1353 and the implementing General Services Administration regulation, as codified under 41 CFR chapter 304, and authorizes an employee to undertake the travel. At the conference the advocacy group, as agreed, pays the employee's hotel bill and provides several of his meals. Subsequently the group reimburses the agency for the cost of the employee's airfare and some additional meals. All of the payments by the advocacy group are permissible. Since the employee is speaking officially and the expense payments are accepted under 31 U.S.C. 1353, they are not prohibited compensation under Section 2635.807(a)(2)(iii). The same result would obtain with respect to expense payments made by non-Government sources properly authorized under an agency gift acceptance statute, the Government Employees Training Act, 5 U.S.C. 4111, or the foreign gifts law, 5 U.S.C. 7342.

(iv) Receive means that there is actual or constructive receipt of the compensation by the employee so that the employee has the right to exercise dominion and control over the compensation and to direct its subsequent use. Compensation received by an employee includes compensation which is:

(A) Paid to another person, including a charitable organization, on the basis of designation, recommendation or other specification by the employee; or

(B) Paid with the employee's knowledge and acquiescence to his parent, sibling, spouse, child, or dependent relative.

(v) Particular matter involving specific parties has the meaning set forth in Section 2637.102(a)(7) of this chapter.

(vi) Personal and substantial participation has the meaning set forth in Section 2635.402(b)(4). (3) Exception for teaching certain courses. Notwithstanding that the activity would relate to his official duties under paragraphs (a) (2)(i) (B) or (E) of this section, an employee may accept compensation for teaching a course requiring multiple presentations by the employee if the course is offered as part of: (i) The regularly established curriculum of: (A) An institution of higher education as defined at 20 U.S.C. 1141(a); (B) An elementary school as defined at 20 U.S.C. 2891(8); or (C) A secondary school as defined at 20 U.S.C. 2891(21); or (ii) A program of education or training sponsored and funded by the Federal Government or by a State or local government which is not offered by an entity described in paragraph (a) (3)(i) of this section.

Example 1: An employee of the Cost Accounting Standards Board who teaches an advanced accounting course as part of the regular business school curriculum of an accredited university may receive compensation for teaching the course even though a substantial portion of the course deals with cost accounting principles applicable to contracts with the Government.

Example 2: An attorney employed by the Equal Employment Opportunity Commission may accept compensation for teaching a course at a state college on the subject of Federal employment discrimination law. The attorney could not accept compensation for teaching the same seminar as part of a continuing education program sponsored by her bar association because the subject of the course is focused on the operations or programs of the EEOC and the sponsor of the course is not an accredited educational institution.

Example 3: An employee of the National Endowment for the Humanities is invited by a private university to teach a course that is a survey of Government policies in support of artists, poets and writers. As part of his official duties, the employee administers a grant that the university has received from the NEH. The employee may not accept compensation for teaching the course because the university has interests that may be substantially affected by the performance or nonperformance of the employee's duties. Likewise, an employee may not receive compensation for any teaching that is undertaken as part of his official duties or that involves the use of nonpublic information.

(b) Reference to official position. An employee who is engaged in teaching, speaking or writing as outside employment or as an outside activity shall not use or permit the use of his official title or position to identify him in connection with his teaching, speaking or writing activity or to promote any book, seminar, course, program or similar undertaking, except that:

(1) An employee may include or permit the inclusion of his title or position as one of several biographical details when such information is given to identify him in connection with his teaching, speaking or writing, provided that his title or position is given no more prominence than other significant biographical details;

(2) An employee may use, or permit the use of, his title or position in connection with an article published in a scientific or professional journal, provided that the title or position is accompanied by a reasonably prominent disclaimer satisfactory to the agency stating that the views expressed in the article do not necessarily represent the views of the agency or the United States; and

(3) An employee who is ordinarily addressed using a general term of address, such as "The Honorable," or a rank, such as a military or ambassadorial rank, may use or permit the use of that term of address or rank in connection with his teaching, speaking or writing.

**Note**: Some agencies may have policies requiring advance agency review, clearance, or approval of certain speeches, books, articles or similar products to determine whether the product contains an appropriate disclaimer, discloses nonpublic information, or otherwise complies with this section.

Example 1: A meteorologist employed with the National Oceanic and Atmospheric Administration is asked by a local university to teach a graduate course on hurricanes. The university may include the meteorologist's Government title and position together with other information about his education and previous employment in course materials setting forth biographical data on all teachers involved in the graduate program. However, his title or position may not be used to promote the course, for example, by featuring the meteorologist's Government title, Senior Meteorologist, NOAA, in bold type under his name. In contrast, his title may be used in this manner when the meteorologist is authorized by NOAA to speak in his official capacity.

Example 2: A doctor just employed by the Centers for Disease Control has written a paper based on his earlier independent research into cell structures. Incident to the paper's publication in the Journal of the American Medical Association, the doctor may be given credit for the paper, as Dr. M. Wellbeing, Associate Director, Centers for Disease Control, provided that the article also contains a disclaimer, concurred in by the CDC, indicating that the paper is the result of the doctor's independent research and does not represent the findings of the CDC.

Example 3: An employee of the Federal Deposit Insurance Corporation has been asked to give a speech in his private capacity, without compensation, to the annual meeting of a committee of the American Bankers Association on the need for banking reform. The employee may be described in his introduction at the meeting as an employee of the Federal Deposit Insurance Corporation provided that other pertinent biographical details are mentioned as well.

**Section 2635.808 Fundraising activities.**

An employee may engage in fundraising only in accordance with the restrictions in part 950 of this title on the conduct of charitable fundraising in the Federal workplace and in accordance with paragraphs (b) and (c) of this section.

(a) **Definitions**. For purposes of this section:

(1) Fundraising means the raising of funds for a nonprofit organization, other than a political organization as defined in 26 U.S.C. 527(e), through:

(i) Solicitation of funds or sale of items; or

(ii) Participation in the conduct of an event by an employee where any portion of the cost of attendance or participation may be taken as a charitable tax deduction by a person incurring that cost.

(2) Participation in the conduct of an event means active and visible participation in the promotion, production, or presentation of the event and includes serving as honorary chairperson, sitting at a head table during the event, and standing in a reception line. The term does not include mere attendance at an event provided that, to the employee's knowledge, his attendance is not used by the nonprofit organization to promote the event. While the term generally includes any public speaking during the event, it does not include the delivery of an official speech as defined in paragraph (a)(3) of this section or any seating or other participation appropriate to the delivery of such a speech. Waiver of a fee for attendance at an event by a participant in the conduct of that event does not constitute a gift for purposes of subpart B of this part.

**Note**: This section does not prohibit fundraising for a political party, candidate for partisan political office, or partisan political group. However, there are statutory restrictions that apply to political fundraising. For example, under the Hatch Act Reform Amendments of 1993, at 5 U.S.C. 7323(a), employees may not knowingly solicit, accept, or receive a political contribution from any person, except under limited circumstances. In addition, employees are prohibited by 18 U.S.C. 607 from soliciting or receiving political contributions in Federal offices, and, except as permitted by the Hatch Act Reform Amendments, are prohibited by 18 U.S.C. 602 from knowingly soliciting political contributions from other employees.

Example 1: The Secretary of Transportation has been asked to serve as master of ceremonies for an All-Star Gala. Tickets to the event cost $150 and are tax deductible as a charitable donation, with proceeds to be donated to a local hospital. By serving as master of ceremonies, the Secretary would be participating in fundraising.

(3) Official speech means a speech given by an employee in his official capacity on a subject matter that relates to his official duties, provided that the employee's agency has determined that the event at which the speech is to be given provides an appropriate forum for the dissemination of the information to be presented and provided that the employee does not request donations or other support for the nonprofit organization. Subject matter relates to an employee's official duties if it focuses specifically on the employee's official duties, on the responsibilities, programs, or operations of the employee's agency as described in Section 2635.807(a)(2)(i)(E), or on matters of Administration policy on which the employee has been authorized to speak.

Example 1: The Secretary of Labor is invited to speak at a banquet honoring a distinguished labor leader, the proceeds of which will benefit a nonprofit organization that assists homeless families. She devotes a major portion of her speech to the Administration's Points of Light initiative, an effort to encourage citizens to volunteer their time to help solve serious social problems. Because she is authorized to speak on Administration policy, her remarks at the banquet are an official speech. However, the Secretary would be engaged in fundraising if she were to conclude her official speech with a request for donations to the nonprofit organization.

Example 2: A charitable organization is sponsoring a two-day tennis tournament at a country club in the Washington, DC area to raise funds for recreational programs for learning disabled children. The organization has invited the Secretary of Education to give a speech on federally funded special education programs at the awards dinner to be held at the conclusion of the tournament and a determination has been made that the dinner is an appropriate forum for the particular speech. The Secretary may speak at the dinner and, under Section 2635.204(g)(1), he may partake of the meal provided to him at the dinner.

(4) Personally solicit means to request or otherwise encourage donations or other support either through person-to-person contact or through the use of one's name or identity in correspondence or by permitting its use by others. It does not include the solicitation of funds through the media or through either oral remarks, or the contemporaneous dispatch of like items of mass- produced correspondence, if such remarks or correspondence are addressed to a group consisting of many persons, unless it is known to the employee that the solicitation is targeted at subordinates or at persons who are prohibited sources within the meaning of Section 2635.203(d). It does not include behind-the-scenes assistance in the solicitation of funds, such as drafting correspondence, stuffing envelopes, or accounting for contributions.

Example 1: An employee of the Department of Energy who signs a letter soliciting funds for a local private school does not "personally solicit" funds when 500 copies of the letter, which makes no mention of his DOE position and title, are mailed to members of the local community, even though some individuals who are employed by Department of Energy contractors may receive the letter.

(b) **Fundraising in an official capacity**. An employee may participate in fundraising in an official capacity if, in accordance with a statute, Executive order, regulation or otherwise as determined by the agency, he is authorized to engage in the fundraising activity as part of his official duties. When authorized to participate in an official capacity, an employee may use his official title, position and authority. Example 1: Because participation in his official capacity is authorized under part 950 of this title, the Secretary of the Army may sign a memorandum to all Army personnel encouraging them to donate to the Combined Federal Campaign.

(c) **Fundraising in a personal capacity**. An employee may engage in fundraising in his personal capacity provided that he does not:

(1) Personally solicit funds or other support from a subordinate or from any person:

(i) Known to the employee, if the employee is other than a special Government employee, to be a prohibited source within the meaning of Section 2635.203(d); or

(ii) Known to the employee, if the employee is a special Government employee, to be a prohibited source within the meaning of Section 2635.203(d)(4) that is a person whose interests may be substantially affected by performance or nonperformance of his official duties.

(2) Use or permit the use of his official title, position or any authority associated with his public office to further the fundraising effort, except that an employee who is ordinarily addressed using a general term of address, such as "The Honorable," or a rank, such as a military or ambassadorial rank, may use or permit the use of that term of address or rank for such purposes; or

(3) Engage in any action that would otherwise violate this part.

Example 1: A nonprofit organization is sponsoring a golf tournament to raise funds for underprivileged children. The Secretary of the Navy may not enter the tournament with the understanding that the organization intends to attract participants by offering other entrants the opportunity, in exchange for a donation in the form of an entry fee, to spend the day playing 18 holes of golf in a foursome with the Secretary of the Navy.

Example 2: An employee of the Merit Systems Protection Board may not use the agency's photocopier to reproduce fundraising literature for her son's private school. Such use of the photocopier would violate the standards at Section 2635.704 regarding use of Government property.

Example 3: An Assistant Attorney General may not sign a letter soliciting funds for a homeless shelter as "John Doe, Assistant Attorney General." He also may not sign a letter with just his signature, "John Doe," soliciting funds from a prohibited source, unless the letter is one of many identical, mass-produced letters addressed to a large group where the solicitation is not known to him to be targeted at persons who are either prohibited sources or subordinates.

# I
# CONFLICTS OF INTEREST

*STANDARD*

Public employees should safeguard their ability to make independent, objective, fair and impartial judgments by scrupulously avoiding financial, social and political relationships and transactions which may compromise or give the appearance of compromising their objectivity, independence or honesty.

Four issues that are related to the stated principle are:

A. *Disclosure of Financial Conflicts of Interest*
B. *Benefits Intended to Influence*
C. *Duty to Report Improper Offers*
D. *Appearance of Undue Influence*

# I(A)
# Disclosure of Financial Conflicts of Interest

*STANDARD*

Public employees subject to disclosure of financial interest requirements should comply with both the letter and spirit of the regulations and not seek to circumvent them by evasion strategies or legalisms.

*GUIDELINES AND COMMENTARY*

*Is It Mandatory to Disclose Financial Matters?*

Under the Executive Order 11222, the Ethics in Government Act, and 5 CFR 735 it is required to file certain statements of employment and financial interest by certain designated employees.

How is the Issue Concerning Financial Conflicts of Interest Addressed?

By far, the most highly regulated area of public service ethics deals with financial conflicts of interest. The dominant method of regulation takes the form of disclosure requirements. These requirements avoid outright prohibition of conflicting interests, allowing public employees to accept a wide variety of benefits as gratuities and earned income so long as the transaction is reported to a designated government agency. The theory is that disclosure permits the public to decide the propriety of the relationship or transaction and hold the official accountable. Such requirements, however, often involve elaborate bureaucratic mechanisms to assure that restricted transactions are properly reported. Usually, these bureaucracies are understaffed and underfunded and they are unable to provide comprehensive and timely audit assurances of the completeness or accuracy of reports.

## *What Is the Consequence?*

Many public employees, as a result of the elaborate bureaucratic mechanisms, are tempted to circumvent the spirit of the regulations by adopting evasion strategies which raise little risk of sanction — late filings, incomplete answers, technical justifications to resist disclosure, etc. The principled public employee should conscientiously overcome these temptations and make full, open, forthright and timely reports, resolving doubts in favor of disclosure.

---

### OGE RULES:

**Section 2635.403 Prohibited financial interests**.

An employee shall not acquire or hold any financial interest that he is prohibited from acquiring or holding by statute, by agency regulation issued in accordance with paragraph (a) of this section or by reason of an agency determination of substantial conflict under paragraph (b) of this section.

**Note**: There is no statute of Governmentwide applicability prohibiting employees from holding or acquiring any financial interest. Statutory restrictions, if any, are contained in agency statutes which, in some cases, may be implemented by agency regulations issued independent of this part.

(a) **Agency regulation prohibiting certain financial interests**. An agency may, by supplemental agency regulation issued after February 3, 1993, prohibit or restrict the acquisition or holding of a financial interest or a class of financial interests by agency employees, or any category of agency employees, and the spouses and minor children of those employees, based

---

on the agency's determination that the acquisition or holding of such financial interests would cause a reasonable person to question the impartiality and objectivity with which agency programs are administered. Where the agency restricts or prohibits the holding of certain financial interests by its employees' spouses or minor children, any such prohibition or restriction shall be based on a determination that there is a direct and appropriate nexus between the prohibition or restriction as applied to spouses and minor children and the efficiency of the service.

(b) **Agency determination of substantial conflict**. An agency may prohibit or restrict an individual employee from acquiring or holding a financial interest or a class of financial interests based upon the agency designee's determination that the holding of such interest or interests will:

(1) Require the employee's disqualification from matters so central or critical to the performance of his official duties that the employee's ability to perform the duties of his position would be materially impaired; or

(2) Adversely affect the efficient accomplishment of the agency's mission because another employee cannot be readily assigned to perform work from which the employee would be disqualified by reason of the financial interest.

Example 1: An Air Force employee who owns stock in a major aircraft engine manufacturer is being considered for promotion to a position that involves responsibility for development of a new fighter airplane. If the agency determined that engineering and other decisions about the Air Force's requirements for the fighter would directly and predictably affect his financial interests, the employee could not, by virtue of 18 U.S.C. 208(a), perform these significant duties of the position while retaining his stock in the company. The agency can require the employee to sell his stock as a condition of being selected for the position rather than allowing him to disqualify himself in particular matters.

(c) **Definition of financial interest**. For purposes of this section:

(1) Except as provided in paragraph (c)(2) of this section, the term financial interest is limited to financial interests that are owned by the employee or by the employee's spouse or minor children. However, the term is not limited to only those financial interests that would be disqualifying under 18 U.S.C. 208(a) and Section 2635.402. The term includes any current or contingent ownership, equity, or security interest in real or personal property or a business and may include an indebtedness or compensated employment relationship. It thus includes, for example, interests in the nature of stocks, bonds, partnership interests, fee and leasehold interests, mineral and other property rights, deeds of trust, and liens, and extends to any right to purchase or acquire any such interest, such as a stock option or commodity future. It does not include a future interest created by someone other than the employee, his spouse, or dependent child or any right as a beneficiary of an estate that has not been settled.

Example 1: A regulatory agency has concluded that ownership by its employees of stock in entities regulated by the agency would significantly diminish public confidence in the agency's performance of its regulatory functions and thereby interfere with the accomplishment of its mission. In its supplemental agency regulations, the agency may prohibit its employees from acquiring or continuing to hold stock in regulated entities.

Example 2: An agency that insures bank deposits may, by supplemental agency regulation, prohibit its employees who are bank examiners from obtaining loans from banks they examine. Examination of a member bank could have no effect on an employee's fixed obligation to repay a loan from that bank and, thus, would not affect an employee's financial interests so as to require disqualification under Section 2635.402. Nevertheless, a loan from a member bank is a discrete financial interest within the meaning of Section 2635.403(c) that may, when appropriate, be prohibited by supplemental agency regulation.

(2) The term financial interest includes service, with or without compensation, as an officer, director, trustee, general partner or employee of any person, including a nonprofit entity, whose financial interests are imputed to the employee

under Section 2635.402(b) (2)(iii) or (iv).

Example 1: The Foundation for the Preservation of Wild Horses maintains herds of horses that graze on public and private lands. Because its costs are affected by Federal policies regarding grazing permits, the Foundation routinely comments on all proposed rules governing use of Federal grasslands issued by the Bureau of Land Management. BLM may require an employee to resign his uncompensated position as Vice President of the Foundation as a condition of his promotion to a policy- level position within the Bureau rather than allowing him to rely on disqualification in particular cases.

(d) **Reasonable period to divest or terminate**. Whenever an agency directs divestiture of a financial interest under paragraph (a) or (b) of this section, the employee shall be given a reasonable period of time, considering the nature of his particular duties and the nature and marketability of the interest, within which to comply with the agency's direction. Except in cases of unusual hardship, as determined by the agency, a reasonable period shall not exceed 90 days from the date divestiture is first directed. However, as long as the employee continues to hold the financial interest, he remains subject to any restrictions imposed by this subpart.

(e) **Eligibility for special tax treatment**. An employee required to sell or otherwise divest a financial interest may be eligible to defer the tax consequences of divestiture under subpart J of part 2634 of this chapter.

# I(B)
## Benefits Intended to Influence

*STANDARD*

Public employees should not accept benefits of any sort from any person under circumstances from which it could be reasonably inferred that the benefit was intended to influence them in the performance of their public duties.

---

**OGE RULES:**

**Section 2635.902(bb)** The prohibitions on disclosing and obtaining certain procurement information (41 U.S.C. 423(a) and (b)).

**Section 2635.902(hh)** The prohibition against solicitation or acceptance of anything of value to obtain public office for another (18 U.S.C. 211).

---

This standard entails three different areas of concern:

1. *Bribery*
2. *Attempts to Influence Public Action*
3. *Impropriety of Accepting Gifts*

*GUIDELINES AND COMMENTARY*

1. *What is Bribery?*

In most jurisdictions, a person commits the crime of bribery if the person provides or offers to provide a benefit to a public employee with the intent to influence the public employee's vote, opinion, judgment, action, decision, or exercise of discretion. The procedural safeguards of a criminal trial, however, including the high standard of proof, make it difficult to establish the crime.

It is critical to recognize that the acceptance by public employees of benefits of any sort from persons who wish to influence official actions raises ethical problems even when the transaction does not rise to the level of bribery. The ethical obligation to avoid transactions which cast doubt on the integrity of government is much more stringent.

2. *What Are Some Types of Benefits Used as Attempts to Influence Action?*

Some ways that are used as attempts to influence public action are by seeking to form relationships with public employees based on personal benefits — jobs, special investment opportunities, loans, travel, lodging, entertainment, gifts, favors, discounts, etc. — which are intended to appeal to self-interest and distract public employees from their commitment to use public powers only to advance public interests. The offer and acceptance of private benefits intended to influence public actions should be avoided scrupulously; it creates real and apparent conflicts of interest.

### 3. *What Is Improper About Accepting Benefits?*

Public employees are obligated to protect the public trust by avoiding both the appearance and the reality of impropriety. Therefore, in accepting any benefit, whether in the form of compensation for services or a gratuity, it is not enough that the public employee has no intent to do anything improper or, in fact, that nothing improper is done. The appearance of impropriety is far too strong to permit acceptance of any benefit arising from a corrupt motive.

# I(C)
# Duty to Report Improper Offers

*STANDARD*

When the possibility of improper motive requires refusal of a gratuity, the official should firmly warn the person about bribery laws and improper influence; if the attempt to unduly influence is clear, the matter should be reported to law enforcement authorities.

*GUIDELINES AND COMMENTARY*

### *Is Saying "No" to Offers Enough?*

It is not always sufficient to turn down an improper offer of gifts or other benefits. Any attempt to unduly influence a public official warrants some action that at least educates the offeror of the impropriety and risk of such conduct.

### *What Actions Should Be Taken When Being Offered Improper Benefits?*

Occasionally, an improper offer is made by an unsophisticated individual who should have, but did not know any better. A polite but firm warning may be sufficient. On the other hand, improperly motivated gratuities are attempted bribes and when the source is politically experienced, the matter should be handled with great seriousness. In some cases, the failure to react with indignation or report improper offers to the authorities can be viewed as wrong in itself.

# I(D)
## Appearance of Undue Influence

*STANDARD*

Regardless of the actual intent of the provider or recipient of a benefit, public employees should not accept benefits of any sort under circumstances which would create in the mind of a reasonable observer the belief the benefit may influence them in the performance of their public responsibilities.

> *"What happens is a gradual shifting of a man's loyalty from the community to those who have been doing him favors. His final decisions, therefore, are made in response to his private friendships and loyalties rather than to the public good. Throughout this whole process an official will claim — and may indeed believe — that there is no causal connection between the favors he has received and the decisions which he makes. . . . [T]he whole process may be so subtle as to not be detected by the official himself."*
> — Senator Paul Douglas

Given the above standard, the following issues are important to consider:

1. *The Factors of a Gift Being Offered*
2. *Whether a Gift Will Or Will Not Impugn Personal Integrity*
3. *If It Matters If the Gift Is Given After An Act*

---

**OGE RULES:**

**Section 2635.101(b)(4)** An employee shall not, except as permitted by subpart B of this part, solicit or accept any gift or other item of monetary value from any person or entity seeking official action from, doing business with, or conducting activities regulated by the employee's agency, or whose interests may be substantially affected by the performance or

---

nonperformance of the employee's duties.

### Section 2635.202

(a) **General prohibitions**. Except as provided in this subpart, an employee shall not, directly or indirectly, solicit or accept a gift:

(1) From a prohibited source; or

(2) Given because of the employee's official position.

(b) **Relationship to illegal gratuities statute**. Unless accepted in violation of paragraph (c)(1) of this section, a gift accepted under the standards set forth in this subpart shall not constitute an illegal gratuity otherwise prohibited by 18 U.S.C. 201(c)(1)(B).

(c) **Limitations on use of exceptions**. Notwithstanding any exception provided in this subpart, other than Section 2635.204(j), an employee shall not:

(1) Accept a gift in return for being influenced in the performance of an official act;

(2) Solicit or coerce the offering of a gift;

(3) Accept gifts from the same or different sources on a basis so frequent that a reasonable person would be led to believe the employee is using his public office for private gain;

Example 1: A purchasing agent for a Veterans Administration hospital routinely deals with representatives of pharmaceutical manufacturers who provide information about new company products. Because of his crowded calendar, the purchasing agent has offered to meet with manufacturer representatives during his lunch hours Tuesdays through Thursdays and the representatives routinely arrive at the employee's office bringing a sandwich and a soft drink for the employee. Even though the market value of each of the lunches is less than $6 and the aggregate value from any one manufacturer does not exceed the $50 aggregate limitation in Section 2635.204(a) on de minimis gifts of $20 or less, the practice of accepting even these modest gifts on a recurring basis is improper.

(4) Accept a gift in violation of any statute. Relevant statutes applicable to all employees include:

(i) 18 U.S.C. 201(b), which prohibits a public official from seeking, accepting, or agreeing to receive or accept anything of value in return for being influenced in the performance of an official act or for being induced to take or omit to take any action in violation of his official duty. As used in 18 U.S.C. 201(b), the term "public official" is broadly construed and includes regular and special Government employees as well as all other Government officials; and

(ii) 18 U.S.C. 209, which prohibits an employee, other than a special Government employee, from receiving any salary or any contribution to or supplementation of salary from any source other than the United States as compensation for services as a Government employee. The statute contains several specific exceptions to this general prohibition, including an exception for contributions made from the treasury of a State, county, or municipality; or

(5) Accept vendor promotional training contrary to applicable regulations, policies or guidance relating to the procurement of supplies and services for the Government, except pursuant to Section 2635.204(l).

### Section 2635.203(b) Definitions

Gift includes any gratuity, favor, discount, entertainment, hospitality, loan, forbearance, or other item having monetary value. It includes services as well as gifts of training, transportation, local travel, lodgings and meals, whether provided in-kind, by purchase of a ticket, payment in advance, or reimbursement after the expense has been incurred. It does not include:

(1) Modest items of food and refreshments, such as soft drinks, coffee and donuts, offered other than as part of a meal;

(2) Greeting cards and items with little intrinsic value, such as plaques, certificates, and trophies, which are intended solely for presentation;

(3) Loans from banks and other financial institutions on terms generally available to the public;

(4) Opportunities and benefits, including favorable rates and commercial discounts, available to the public or to a class consisting of all Government employees or all uniformed military personnel, whether or not restricted on the basis of geographic considerations;

(5) Rewards and prizes given to competitors in contests or events, including random drawings, open to the public unless the employee's entry into the contest or event is required as part of his official duties;

(6) Pension and other benefits resulting from continued participation in an employee welfare and benefits plan maintained by a former employer;

(7) Anything which is paid for by the Government or secured by the Government under Government contract; Note: Some airlines encourage those purchasing tickets to join programs that award free flights and other benefits to frequent fliers. Any such benefit earned on the basis of Government- financed travel belongs to the agency rather than to the employee and may be accepted only insofar as provided under 41 CFR part 301-53.

(8) Any gift accepted by the Government under specific statutory authority, including:

(i) Travel, subsistence, and related expenses accepted by an agency under the authority of 31 U.S.C. 1353 in connection with an employee's attendance at a meeting or similar function relating to his official duties which takes place away from his duty station. The agency's acceptance must be in accordance with the implementing regulations at 41 CFR part 304-1; and

(ii) Other gifts provided in-kind which have been accepted by an agency under its agency gift acceptance statute; or (9) Anything for which market value is paid by the employee. (c) Market value means the retail cost the employee would incur to purchase the gift. An employee who cannot ascertain the market value of a gift may estimate its market value by reference to the retail cost of similar items of like quality. The market value of a gift of a ticket entitling the holder to food, refreshments, entertainment, or any other benefit shall be the face value of the ticket.

Example 1: An employee who has been given an acrylic paperweight embedded with the corporate logo of a prohibited source may determine its market value based on her observation that a comparable acrylic paperweight, not embedded with a logo, generally sells for about $20.

Example 2: A prohibited source has offered an employee a ticket to a charitable event consisting of a cocktail reception to be followed by an evening of chamber music. Even though the food, refreshments, and entertainment provided at the event may be worth only $20, the market value of the ticket is its $250 face value.

(d) Prohibited source means any person who:

(1) Is seeking official action by the employee's agency;

(2) Does business or seeks to do business with the employee's agency;

(3) Conducts activities regulated by the employee's agency;

(4) Has interests that may be substantially affected by performance or nonperformance of the employee's official duties; or

(5) Is an organization a majority of whose members are described in paragraphs (d) (1) through (4) of this section.

(e) A gift is solicited or accepted because of the employee's official position if it is from a person other than an employee and would not have been solicited, offered, or given had the employee not held the status, authority or duties associated with his Federal position. Note: Gifts between employees are subject to the limitations set forth in subpart C of this part.

Example 1: Where free season tickets are offered by an opera guild to all members of the Cabinet, the gift is offered because of their official positions.

Example 2. Employees at a regional office of the Department of Justice (DOJ) work in Government-leased space at a private office building, along with various private business tenants. A major fire in the building during normal office hours causes a traumatic experience for all occupants of the building in making their escape, and it is the subject of widespread news coverage. A corporate hotel chain, which does not meet the definition of a prohibited source for DOJ, seizes the moment and announces that it will give a free night's lodging to all building occupants and their families, as a public goodwill gesture. Employees of DOJ may accept, as this gift is not being given because of their Government positions. The donor's motivation for offering this gift is unrelated to the DOJ employees' status, authority or duties associated with their Federal position, but instead is based on their mere presence in the building as occupants at the time of the fire.

(f) A gift which is solicited or accepted indirectly includes a gift:

(1) Given with the employee's knowledge and acquiescence to his parent, sibling, spouse, child, or dependent relative because of that person's relationship to the employee, or

(2) Given to any other person, including any charitable organization, on the basis of designation, recommendation, or other specification by the employee, except as permitted for the disposition of perishable items by Section 2635.205(a)(2) or for payments made to charitable organizations in lieu of honoraria under Section 2636.204 of this chapter.

Example 1: An employee who must decline a gift of a personal computer pursuant to this subpart may not suggest that the gift be given instead to one of five charitable organizations whose names are provided by the employee.

(g) Vendor promotional training means training provided by any person for the purpose of promoting its products or services. It does not include training provided under a Government contract or by a contractor to facilitate use of products or services it furnishes under a Government contract.

### Section 2635.204 Exceptions.

The prohibitions set forth in Section 2635.202(a) do not apply to a gift accepted under the circumstances described in paragraphs (a) through (l) of this section, and an employee's acceptance of a gift in accordance with one of those paragraphs will be deemed not to violate the principles set forth in Section 2635.101(b), including appearances. Even though acceptance of a gift may be permitted by one of the exceptions contained in paragraphs (a) through (l) of this section, it is never inappropriate and frequently prudent for an employee to decline a gift offered by a prohibited source or because of his official position.

(a) **Gifts of $20 or less**. An employee may accept unsolicited gifts having an aggregate market value of $20 or less per source per occasion, provided that the aggregate market value of individual gifts received from any one person under the authority of this paragraph shall not exceed $50 in a calendar year. This exception does not apply to gifts of cash or of investment interests such as stock, bonds, or certificates of deposit. Where the market value of a gift or the aggregate market value of gifts offered on any single occasion exceeds $20, the employee may not pay the excess value over $20 in order to accept that portion of the gift or those gifts worth $20. Where the aggregate value of tangible items offered on a single occasion exceeds $20, the employee may decline any distinct and separate item in order to accept those items aggregating $20 or less.

Example 1: An employee of the Securities and Exchange Commission and his spouse have been invited by a representative of a regulated entity to a Broadway play, tickets to which have a face value of $30 each. The aggregate market value of the gifts offered on this single occasion is $60, $40 more than the $20 amount that may be accepted for a single event or presentation. The employee may not accept the gift of the evening of entertainment. He and his spouse may attend the play only if he pays the full $60 value of the two tickets.

Example 2: An employee of the Defense Mapping Agency has been invited by an association of cartographers to speak about his agency's role in the evolution of missile technology. At the conclusion of his speech, the association presents the employee a framed map with a market value of $18 and a book about the history of cartography with a market value of $15. The employee may accept the map or the book, but not both, since the aggregate value of these two tangible items exceeds $20.

Example 3: On four occasions during the calendar year, an employee of the Defense Logistics Agency was given gifts worth $10 each by four employees of a corporation that is a DLA contractor. For purposes of applying the yearly $50 limitation on gifts of $20 or less from any one person, the four gifts must be aggregated because a person is defined at Section 2635.102(k) to mean not only the corporate entity, but its officers and employees as well. However, for purposes of applying the $50 aggregate limitation, the employee would not have to include the value of a birthday present received from his cousin, who is employed by the same corporation, if he can accept the birthday present under the exception at Section 2635.204(b) for gifts based on a personal relationship.

Example 4: Under the authority of 31 U.S.C. 1353 for agencies to accept payments from non-Federal sources in connection with attendance at certain meetings or similar functions, the Environmental Protection Agency has accepted an association's gift of travel expenses and conference fees for an employee of its Office of Radiation Programs to attend an international conference on "The Chernobyl Experience." While at the conference, the employee may accept a gift of $20 or less from the association or from another person attending the conference even though it was not approved in advance by the EPA. Although 31 U.S.C. 1353 is the only authority under which an agency may accept gifts from certain non-Federal sources in connection with its employees' attendance at such functions, a gift of $20 or less accepted under Section 2635.204(a) is a gift to the employee rather than to his employing agency.

Example 5: During off-duty time, an employee of the Department of Defense (DOD) attends a trade show involving companies that are DOD contractors. He is offered a $15 computer program disk at X Company's booth, a $12 appointments calendar at Y Company's booth, and a deli lunch worth $8 from Z Company. The employee may accept all three of these items because they do not exceed $20 per source, even though they total more than $20 at this single occasion.

(b) **Gifts based on a personal relationship**. An employee may accept a gift given under circumstances which make it clear that the gift is motivated by a family relationship or personal friendship rather than the position of the employee. Relevant factors in making such a determination include the history of the relationship and whether the family member or friend personally pays for the gift.

Example 1: An employee of the Federal Deposit Insurance Corporation has been dating a secretary employed by a member bank. For Secretary's Week, the bank has given each secretary 2 tickets to an off-Broadway musical review and has urged each to invite a family member or friend to share the evening of entertainment. Under the circumstances, the FDIC employee may accept his girlfriend's invitation to the theater. Even though the tickets were initially purchased by the member bank, they were given without reservation to the secretary to use as she wished, and her invitation to the employee was motivated by their personal friendship.

Example 2: Three partners in a law firm that handles corporate mergers have invited an employee of the Federal Trade Commission to join them in a golf tournament at a private club at the firm's expense. The entry fee is $500 per foursome. The employee cannot accept the gift of one- quarter of the entry fee even though he and the three partners have developed an amicable relationship as a result of the firm's dealings with the FTC. As evidenced in part by the fact that the fees are to be paid by the firm, it is not a personal friendship but a business relationship that is the motivation behind the partners' gift.

(c) **Discounts and similar benefits**. In addition to those opportunities and benefits excluded from the definition of a gift by Section 2635.203(b)(4), an employee may accept:

(1) Reduced membership or other fees for participation in organization activities offered to all Government employees or all uniformed military personnel by professional organizations if the only restrictions on membership relate to professional qualifications; and

(2) Opportunities and benefits, including favorable rates and commercial discounts not precluded by paragraph (c)(3) of this section:

(i) Offered to members of a group or class in which membership is unrelated to Government employment;

(ii) Offered to members of an organization, such as an employees' association or agency credit union, in which membership is related to Government employment if the same offer is broadly available to large segments of the public through organizations of similar size; or

(iii) Offered by a person who is not a prohibited source to any group or class that is not defined in a manner that specifically discriminates among Government employees on the basis of type of official responsibility or on a basis that favors those of higher rank or rate of pay; provided, however, that

(3) An employee may not accept for personal use any benefit to which the Government is entitled as the result of an expenditure of Government funds.

Example 1: An employee of the Consumer Product Safety Commission may accept a discount of $50 on a microwave oven offered by the manufacturer to all members of the CPSC employees' association. Even though the CPSC is currently conducting studies on the safety of microwave ovens, the $50 discount is a standard offer that the manufacturer has made broadly available through a number of similar organizations to large segments of the public.

Example 2: An Assistant Secretary may not accept a local country club's offer of membership to all members of Department Secretariats which includes a waiver of its $5,000 membership initiation fee. Even though the country club is not a prohibited source, the offer discriminates in favor of higher ranking officials.

Example 3: The administrative officer for a district office of the Immigration and Naturalization Service has signed an INS order to purchase 50 boxes of photocopy paper from a supplier whose literature advertises that it will give a free briefcase to anyone who purchases 50 or more boxes. Because the paper was purchased with INS funds, the administrative officer cannot keep the briefcase which, if claimed and received, is Government property.

(d) **Awards and honorary degrees**.

(1) An employee may accept gifts, other than cash or an investment interest, with an aggregate market value of $200 or less if such gifts are a bona fide award or incident to a bona fide award that is given for meritorious public service or achievement by a person who does not have interests that may be substantially affected by the performance or nonperformance of the employee's official duties or by an association or other organization the majority of whose members do not have such interests. Gifts with an aggregate market value in excess of $200 and awards of cash or investment interests offered by such persons as awards or incidents of awards that are given for these purposes may be accepted upon a written determination by an agency ethics official that the award is made as part of an established program of recognition:

(i) Under which awards have been made on a regular basis or which is funded, wholly or in part, to ensure its continuation on a regular basis; and

(ii) Under which selection of award recipients is made pursuant to written standards.

(2) An employee may accept an honorary degree from an institution of higher education as defined at 20 U.S.C. 1141(a) based on a written determination by an agency ethics official that the timing of the award of the degree would not cause a reasonable person to question the employee's impartiality in a matter affecting the institution.

(3) An employee who may accept an award or honorary degree pursuant to paragraph (d)(1) or (2) of this section may also accept meals and entertainment given to him and to members of his family at the event at which the presentation takes place.

Example 1: Based on a determination by an agency ethics official that the prize meets the criteria set forth in Section

2635.204(d)(1), an employee of the National Institutes of Health may accept the Nobel Prize for Medicine, including the cash award which accompanies the prize, even though the prize was conferred on the basis of laboratory work performed at NIH.

Example 2: Prestigious University wishes to give an honorary degree to the Secretary of Labor. The Secretary may accept the honorary degree only if an agency ethics official determines in writing that the timing of the award of the degree would not cause a reasonable person to question the Secretary's impartiality in a matter affecting the university.

Example 3: An ambassador selected by a nonprofit organization as recipient of its annual award for distinguished service in the interest of world peace may, together with his wife, and children, attend the awards ceremony dinner and accept a crystal bowl worth $200 presented during the ceremony. However, where the organization has also offered airline tickets for the ambassador and his family to travel to the city where the awards ceremony is to be held, the aggregate value of the tickets and the crystal bowl exceeds $200 and he may accept only upon a written determination by the agency ethics official that the award is made as part of an established program of recognition.

(e) **Gifts based on outside business or employment relationships**. An employee may accept meals, lodgings, transportation and other benefits:

(1) Resulting from the business or employment activities of an employee's spouse when it is clear that such benefits have not been offered or enhanced because of the employee's official position;

Example 1: A Department of Agriculture employee whose husband is a computer programmer employed by an Agriculture Department contractor may attend the company's annual retreat for all of its employees and their families held at a resort facility. However, under Section 2635.502, the employee may be disqualified from performing official duties affecting her husband's employer.

Example 2: Where the spouses of other clerical personnel

have not been invited, an employee of the Defense Contract Audit Agency whose wife is a clerical worker at a defense contractor may not attend the contractor's annual retreat in Hawaii for corporate officers and members of the board of directors, even though his wife received a special invitation for herself and her spouse.

(2) Resulting from his outside business or employment activities when it is clear that such benefits have not been offered or enhanced because of his official status; or

Example 1: The members of an Army Corps of Engineers environmental advisory committee that meets 6 times per year are special Government employees. A member who has a consulting business may accept an invitation to a $50 dinner from her corporate client, an Army construction contractor, unless, for example, the invitation was extended in order to discuss the activities of the committee.

(3) Customarily provided by a prospective employer in connection with bona fide employment discussions. If the prospective employer has interests that could be affected by performance or nonperformance of the employee's duties, acceptance is permitted only if the employee first has complied with the disqualification requirements of subpart F of this part applicable when seeking employment.

Example 1: An employee of the Federal Communications Commission with responsibility for drafting regulations affecting all cable television companies wishes to apply for a job opening with a cable television holding company. Once she has properly disqualified herself from further work on the regulations as required by subpart F of this part, she may enter into employment discussions with the company and may accept the company's offer to pay for her airfare, hotel and meals in connection with an interview trip.

(4) For purposes of paragraphs (e)(1) through (3) of this section, employment shall have the meaning set forth in Section 2635.603(a).

(f) **Gifts in connection with political activities permitted by the Hatch Act Reform Amendments**. An employee who, in accordance with the Hatch Act Reform Amendments of

1993, at 5 U.S.C. 7323, may take an active part in political management or in political campaigns, may accept meals, lodgings, transportation and other benefits, including free attendance at events, when provided, in connection with such active participation, by a political organization described in 26 U.S.C. 527(e). Any other employee, such as a security officer, whose official duties require him to accompany an employee to a political event may accept meals, free attendance and entertainment provided at the event by such an organization.

Example 1: The Secretary of the Department of Health and Human Services may accept an airline ticket and hotel accommodations furnished by the campaign committee of a candidate for the United States Senate in order to give a speech in support of the candidate.

(g) **Widely attended gatherings and other events**

(1) **Speaking and similar engagements**. When an employee is assigned to participate as a speaker or panel participant or otherwise to present information on behalf of the agency at a conference or other event, his acceptance of an offer of free attendance at the event on the day of his presentation is permissible when provided by the sponsor of the event. The employee's participation in the event on that day is viewed as a customary and necessary part of his performance of the assignment and does not involve a gift to him or to the agency.

(2) **Widely attended gatherings**. When there has been a determination that his attendance is in the interest of the agency because it will further agency programs and operations, an employee may accept an unsolicited gift of free attendance at all or appropriate parts of a widely attended gathering of mutual interest to a number of parties from the sponsor of the event or, if more than 100 persons are expected to attend the event and the gift of free attendance has a market value of $285 or less, from a person other than the sponsor of the event. A gathering is widely attended if it is expected that a large number of persons will attend and that persons with a diversity of views or interests will be present, for example, if it is open to members from throughout the interested industry or profession or if those

in attendance represent a range of persons interested in a given matter. For employees subject to a leave system, attendance at the event shall be on the employee's own time or, if authorized by the employee's agency, on excused absence pursuant to applicable guidelines for granting such absence, or otherwise without charge to the employee's leave account.

(3) **Determination of agency interest**. The determination of agency interest required by paragraph (g)(2) of this section shall be made orally or in writing by the agency designee.

(i) If the person who has extended the invitation has interests that may be substantially affected by the performance or nonperformance of an employee's official duties or is an association or organization the majority of whose members have such interests, the employee's participation may be determined to be in the interest of the agency only where there is a written finding by the agency designee that the agency's interest in the employee's participation in the event outweighs the concern that acceptance of the gift of free attendance may or may not appear to improperly influence the employee in the performance of his official duties. Relevant factors that should be considered by the agency designee include the importance of the event to the agency, the nature and sensitivity of any pending matter affecting the interests of the person who has extended the invitation, the significance of the employee's role in any such matter, the purpose of the event, the identity of other expected participants and the market value of the gift of free attendance.

(ii) A blanket determination of agency interest may be issued to cover all or any category of invitees other than those as to whom the finding is required by paragraph (g)(3)(i) of this section. Where a finding under paragraph (g)(3)(i) of this section is required, a written determination of agency interest, including the necessary finding, may be issued to cover two or more employees whose duties similarly affect the interests of the person who has extended the invitation or, where that person is an association or organization, of its members.

(4) **Free attendance**. For purposes of paragraphs (g)(1) and (g)(2) of this section, free attendance may include waiver of all or part of a conference or other fee or the provision of food, refreshments, entertainment, instruction and materials furnished to all attendees as an integral part of the event. It does not include travel expenses, lodgings, entertainment collateral to the event, or meals taken other than in a group setting with all other attendees. Where the invitation has been extended to an accompanying spouse or other guest (see paragraph (g)(6) of this section), the market value of the gift of free attendance includes the market value of free attendance by the spouse or other guest as well as the market value of the employee's own attendance.

**Note**: There are statutory authorities implemented other than by part 2635 under which an agency or an employee may be able to accept free attendance or other items not included in the definition of free attendance, such as travel expenses.

(5) **Cost provided by sponsor of event**. The cost of the employee's attendance will not be considered to be provided by the sponsor, and the invitation is not considered to be from the sponsor of the event, where a person other than the sponsor designates the employee to be invited and bears the cost of the employee's attendance through a contribution or other payment intended to facilitate that employee's attendance. Payment of dues or a similar assessment to a sponsoring organization does not constitute a payment intended to facilitate a particular employee's attendance.

(6) **Accompanying spouse or other guest**. When others in attendance will generally be accompanied by a spouse or other guest, and where the invitation is from the same person who has invited the employee, the agency designee may authorize an employee to accept an unsolicited invitation of free attendance to an accompanying spouse or to another accompanying guest to participate in all or a portion of the event at which the employee's free attendance is permitted under paragraph (g)(1) or (g)(2) of this section. The authorization required by this paragraph may be provided orally or in writing.

Example 1: An aerospace industry association that is a prohibited source sponsors an industrywide, two-day seminar for which it charges a fee of $400 and anticipates attendance of approximately 400. An Air Force contractor pays $2,000 to the association so that the association can extend free invitations to five Air Force officials designated by the contractor. The Air Force officials may not accept the gifts of free attendance. Because the contractor specified the invitees and bore the cost of their attendance, the gift of free attendance is considered to be provided by the company and not by the sponsoring association. Had the contractor paid $2,000 to the association in order that the association might invite any five Federal employees, an Air Force official to whom the sponsoring association extended one of the five invitations could attend if his participation were determined to be in the interest of the agency. The Air Force official could not in any case accept an invitation directly from the nonsponsor contractor because the market value of the gift exceeds $285.

Example 2: An employee of the Department of Transportation is invited by a news organization to an annual press dinner sponsored by an association of press organizations. Tickets for the event cost $285 per person and attendance is limited to 400 representatives of press organizations and their guests. If the employee's attendance is determined to be in the interest of the agency, she may accept the invitation from the news organization because more than 100 persons will attend and the cost of the ticket does not exceed $285. However, if the invitation were extended to the employee and an accompanying guest, her guest could not be authorized to attend for free since the market value of the gift of free attendance would be $570 and the invitation is from a person other than the sponsor of the event.

Example 3: An employee of the Department of Energy (DOE) and his wife have been invited by a major utility executive to a small dinner party. A few other officials of the utility and their spouses or other guests are also invited, as is a representative of a consumer group concerned with utility rates and her husband. The DOE official believes the dinner party will provide him an opportunity to socialize with and get to know those in attendance. The employee may not accept the free invitation under this exception, even if his attendance could be determined to be in the interest of the agency. The small dinner party is not a widely attended gathering. Nor could the employee be authorized to accept even if the event were instead a corporate banquet to which forty company officials and their spouses or other guests were invited. In this second case, notwithstanding the larger number of persons expected (as opposed to the small dinner party just noted) and despite the presence of the consumer group representative and her husband who are not officials of the utility, those in attendance would still not represent a diversity of views or interests. Thus, the company banquet would not qualify as a widely attended gathering under those circumstances either.

Example 4: An employee of the Department of the Treasury authorized to participate in a panel discussion of economic issues as part of a one-day conference may accept the sponsor's waiver of the conference fee. Under the separate authority of Section 2635.204(a), he may accept a token of appreciation for his speech having a market value of $20 or less.

Example 5: An Assistant U.S. Attorney is invited to attend a luncheon meeting of a local bar association to hear a distinguished judge lecture on cross-examining expert witnesses. Although members of the bar association are assessed a $15 fee for the meeting, the Assistant U.S. Attorney may accept the bar association's offer to attend for free, even without a determination of agency interest. The gift can be accepted under the $20 de minimis exception at Section 2635.204(a).

Example 6: An employee of the Department of the Interior authorized to speak on the first day of a four-day conference on endangered species may accept the sponsor's waiver of the conference fee for the first day of the conference. If the conference is widely attended, he may be authorized, based on a determination that his attendance is in the agency's interest, to accept the sponsor's offer to waive the attendance fee for the remainder of the conference.

(h) **Social invitations from persons other than prohibited sources**. An employee may accept food, refreshments and entertainment, not including travel or lodgings, at a social event attended by several persons where:

(1) The invitation is from a person who is not a prohibited source; and

(2) No fee is charged to any person in attendance.

Example 1: Along with several other Government officials and a number of individuals from the private sector, the Administrator of the Environmental Protection Agency has been invited to the premier showing of a new adventure movie about industrial espionage. The producer is paying all costs of the showing. The Administrator may accept the invitation since the producer is not a prohibited source and no attendance fee is being charged to anyone who has been invited.

Example 2: An employee of the White House Press Office has been invited to a cocktail party given by a noted Washington hostess who is not a prohibited source. The employee may attend even though he has only recently been introduced to the hostess and suspects that he may have been invited because of his official position.

(i) **Meals, refreshments and entertainment in foreign areas**. An employee assigned to duty in, or on official travel to, a foreign area as defined in 41 CFR 301-7.3(c) may accept food, refreshments or entertainment in the course of a breakfast, luncheon, dinner or other meeting or event provided:

(1) The market value in the foreign area of the food, refreshments or entertainment provided at the meeting or event, as converted to U.S. dollars, does not exceed the per diem rate for the foreign area specified in the U.S. Department of State's Maximum Per Diem Allowances for Foreign Areas, Per Diem Supplement Section 925 to the Standardized Regulations (GC, FA) available from the Superintendent of Documents, U.S. Government Printing Office, Washington, DC 20402;

(2) There is participation in the meeting or event by non-U.S. citizens or by representatives of foreign governments or other foreign entities;

(3) Attendance at the meeting or event is part of the

employee's official duties to obtain information, disseminate information, promote the export of U.S. goods and services, represent the United States or otherwise further programs or operations of the agency or the U.S. mission in the foreign area; and

(4) The gift of meals, refreshments or entertainment is from a person other than a foreign government as defined in 5 U.S.C. 7342(a)(2). Example 1: A number of local businessmen in a developing country are anxious for a U.S. company to locate a manufacturing facility in their province. An official of the Overseas Private Investment Corporation may accompany the visiting vice president of the U.S. company to a dinner meeting hosted by the businessmen at a province restaurant where the market value of the food and refreshments does not exceed the per diem rate for that country.

(j) **Gifts to the President or Vice President**. Because of considerations relating to the conduct of their offices, including those of protocol and etiquette, the President or the Vice President may accept any gift on his own behalf or on behalf of any family member, provided that such acceptance does not violate Section 2635.202(c) (1) or (2), 18 U.S.C. 201(b) or 201(c)(3), or the Constitution of the United States.

(k) **Gifts authorized by supplemental agency regulation**. An employee may accept any gift the acceptance of which is specifically authorized by a supplemental agency regulation.

(l) **Gifts accepted under specific statutory authority**. The prohibitions on acceptance of gifts from outside sources contained in this subpart do not apply to any item, receipt of which is specifically authorized by statute. Gifts which may be received by an employee under the authority of specific statutes include, but are not limited to:

(1) Free attendance, course or meeting materials, transportation, lodgings, food and refreshments or reimbursements therefor incident to training or meetings when accepted by the employee under the authority of 5 U.S.C. 4111 from an organization with tax-exempt status under 26 U.S.C. 501(c) (3) or from a person to whom the prohibitions in 18 U.S.C. 209 do not apply. The employee's

acceptance must be approved by the agency in accordance with part 410 of this title; or

**Note**: 26 U.S.C. 501(c)(3) is authority for tax-exempt treatment of a limited class of nonprofit organizations, including those organized and operated for charitable, religious or educational purposes. Many nonprofit organizations are not exempt from taxation under this section.

(2) Gifts from a foreign government or international or multinational organization, or its representative, when accepted by the employee under the authority of the Foreign Gifts and Decorations Act, 5 U.S.C. 7342. As a condition of acceptance, an employee must comply with requirements imposed by the agency's regulations or procedures implementing that Act.

**Section 2635.205 Proper disposition of prohibited gifts**.

(a) An employee who has received a gift that cannot be accepted under this subpart shall, unless the gift is accepted by an agency acting under specific statutory authority:

(1) Return any tangible item to the donor or pay the donor its market value. An employee who cannot ascertain the actual market value of an item may estimate its market value by reference to the retail cost of similar items of like quality. See Section 2635.203(c).

Example 1: To avoid public embarrassment to the seminar sponsor, an employee of the National Park Service did not decline a barometer worth $200 given at the conclusion of his speech on Federal lands policy. The employee must either return the barometer or promptly reimburse the sponsor $200.

(2) When it is not practical to return a tangible item because it is perishable, the item may, at the discretion of the employee's supervisor or an agency ethics official, be given to an appropriate charity, shared within the recipient's office, or destroyed.

Example 1: With approval by the recipient's supervisor, a floral arrangement sent by a disability claimant to a helpful employee of the Social Security Administration may be placed in the office's reception area.

(3) For any entertainment, favor, service, benefit or other intangible, reimburse the donor the market value. Subsequent reciprocation by the employee does not constitute reimbursement. Example 1: A Department of Defense employee wishes to attend a charitable event to which he has been offered a $300 ticket by a prohibited source. Although his attendance is not in the interest of the agency under Section 2635.204(g), he may attend if he reimburses the donor the $300 face value of the ticket.

(4) Dispose of gifts from foreign governments or international organizations in accordance with 41 CFR part 101-49, and dispose of materials received in conjunction with official travel in accordance with 41 CFR 101-25.103.

(b) An agency may authorize disposition or return of gifts at Government expense. Employees may use penalty mail to forward reimbursements required or permitted by this section.

(c) An employee who, on his own initiative, promptly complies with the requirements of this section will not be deemed to have improperly accepted an unsolicited gift. An employee who promptly consults his agency ethics official to determine whether acceptance of an unsolicited gift is proper and who, upon the advice of the ethics official, returns the gift or otherwise disposes of the gift in accordance with this section, will be considered to have complied with the requirements of this section on his own initiative.

## SUBPART C - Gifts Between Employees

**Section 2635.301 Overview**. This subpart contains standards that prohibit an employee from giving, donating to, or soliciting contributions for, a gift to an official superior and from accepting a gift from an employee receiving less pay than himself, unless the item is excluded from the definition of a gift or falls within one of the exceptions set forth in this subpart.

**Section 2635.302 General standards**.

(a) **Gifts to superiors**. Except as provided in this subpart, an employee may not: (1) Directly or indirectly, give a gift to or make a donation toward a gift for an official superior; or (2) Solicit a contribution from another employee for a gift to either his own or the other employee's official superior.

(b) **Gifts from employees receiving less pay**. Except as provided in this subpart, an employee may not, directly or indirectly, accept a gift from an employee receiving less pay than himself unless:

(1) The two employees are not in a subordinate-official superior relationship; and

(2) There is a personal relationship between the two employees that would justify the gift.

(c) **Limitation on use of exceptions**. Notwithstanding any exception provided in this subpart, an official superior shall not coerce the offering of a gift from a subordinate.

**Section 2635.303 Definitions**.

For purposes of this subpart, the following definitions shall apply:

(a) Gift has the meaning set forth in Section 2635.203

(b). For purposes of that definition an employee will be deemed to have paid market value for any benefit received as a result of his participation in any carpool or other such mutual arrangement involving another employee or other employees if he bears his fair proportion of the expense or effort involved. (b) Indirectly, for purposes of Section 2635.302(b), has the meaning set forth in Section 2635.203(f). For purposes of Section 2635.302(a), it includes a gift:

(1) Given with the employee's knowledge and acquiescence by his parent, sibling, spouse, child, or dependent relative; or

(2) Given by a person other than the employee under circumstances where the employee has promised or agreed

to reimburse that person or to give that person something of value in exchange for giving the gift.

(c) Subject to paragraph (a) of this section, market value has the meaning set forth in Section 2635.203(c).

(d) Official superior means any other employee, other than the President and the Vice President, including but not limited to an immediate supervisor, whose official responsibilities include directing or evaluating the performance of the employee's official duties or those of any other official superior of the employee. For purposes of this subpart, an employee is considered to be the subordinate of any of his official superiors.

(e) Solicit means to request contributions by personal communication or by general announcement.

(f) Voluntary contribution means a contribution given freely, without pressure or coercion. A contribution is not voluntary unless it is made in an amount determined by the contributing employee, except that where an amount for a gift is included in the cost for a luncheon, reception or similar event, an employee who freely chooses to pay a proportionate share of the total cost in order to attend will be deemed to have made a voluntary contribution. Except in the case of contributions for a gift included in the cost of a luncheon, reception or similar event, a statement that an employee may choose to contribute less or not at all shall accompany any recommendation of an amount to be contributed for a gift to an official superior.

Example 1: A supervisory employee of the Agency for International Development has just been reassigned from Washington, DC to Kabul, Afghanistan. As a farewell party, 12 of her subordinates have decided to take her out to lunch at the Khyber Repast. It is understood that each will pay for his own meal and that the cost of the supervisor's lunch will be divided equally among the twelve. Even though the amount they will contribute is not determined until the supervisor orders lunch, the contribution made by those who choose to participate in the farewell lunch is voluntary.

**Section 2635.304 Exceptions**. The prohibitions set forth in Section 2635.302(a) and (b) do not apply to a gift given or accepted under the circumstances described in paragraph (a) or (b) of this section. A contribution or the solicitation of a contribution that would otherwise violate the prohibitions set forth in Section 2635.302(a) and (b) may only be made in accordance with paragraph (c) of this section.

(a) **General exceptions**. On an occasional basis, including any occasion on which gifts are traditionally given or exchanged, the following may be given to an official superior or accepted from a subordinate or other employee receiving less pay:

(1) Items, other than cash, with an aggregate market value of $10 or less per occasion;

(2) Items such as food and refreshments to be shared in the office among several employees;

(3) Personal hospitality provided at a residence which is of a type and value customarily provided by the employee to personal friends;

(4) Items given in connection with the receipt of personal hospitality if of a type and value customarily given on such occasions; and

(5) Leave transferred under subpart I of part 630 of this title to an employee who is not an immediate supervisor, unless obtained in violation of Section 630.912 of this title.

Example 1: Upon returning to work following a vacation at the beach, a claims examiner with the Department of Veterans Affairs may give his supervisor, and his supervisor may accept, a bag of saltwater taffy purchased on the boardwalk for $8.

Example 2: An employee of the Federal Deposit Insurance Corporation whose bank examination responsibilities require frequent travel may not bring her supervisor, and her supervisor may not accept, souvenir coffee mugs from each of the cities she visits in the course of performing her duties, even though each of the mugs costs less than $5. Gifts given on this basis are not occasional.

Example 3: The Secretary of Labor has invited the agency's General Counsel to a dinner party at his home. The General Counsel may bring a $15 bottle of wine to the dinner party and the Secretary may accept this customary hostess gift from his subordinate, even though its cost is in excess of $10.

Example 4: For Christmas, a secretary may give his supervisor, and the supervisor may accept, a poinsettia plant purchased for $10 or less. The secretary may also invite his supervisor to a Christmas party in his home and the supervisor may attend.

(b) **Special, infrequent occasions.** A gift appropriate to the occasion may be given to an official superior or accepted from a subordinate or other employee receiving less pay:

(1) In recognition of infrequently occurring occasions of personal significance such as marriage, illness, or the birth or adoption of a child; or

(2) Upon occasions that terminate a subordinate-official superior relationship, such as retirement, resignation, or transfer.

Example 1: The administrative assistant to the personnel director of the Tennessee Valley Authority may send a $30 floral arrangement to the personnel director who is in the hospital recovering from surgery. The personnel director may accept the gift.

Example 2: A chemist employed by the Food and Drug Administration has been invited to the wedding of the lab director who is his official superior. He may give the lab director and his bride, and they may accept, a place setting in the couple's selected china pattern purchased for $70.

Example 3: Upon the occasion of the supervisor's retirement from Federal service, an employee of the Fish and Wildlife Service may give her supervisor a book of wildlife photographs which she purchased for $19. The retiring supervisor may accept the book.

(c) **Voluntary contributions**. An employee may solicit voluntary contributions of nominal amounts from fellow employees for an appropriate gift to an official superior and an employee may make a voluntary contribution of a nominal amount to an appropriate gift to an official superior:

(1) On a special, infrequent occasion as described in paragraph (b) of this section; or

(2) On an occasional basis, for items such as food and refreshments to be shared in the office among several employees.

An employee may accept such gifts to which a subordinate or other employee receiving less pay than himself has contributed.

Example 1: To mark the occasion of his retirement, members of the immediate staff of the Under Secretary of the Army would like to give him a party and provide him with a gift certificate. They may distribute an announcement of the party and include a nominal amount for a retirement gift in the fee for the party.

Example 2: The General Counsel of the National Endowment for the Arts may not collect contributions for a Christmas gift for the Chairman. Christmas occurs annually and is not an occasion of personal significance.

Example 3: Subordinates may not take up a collection for a gift to an official superior on the occasion of the superior's swearing in or promotion to a higher grade position within the supervisory chain of that organization. These are not events that mark the termination of the subordinate-official superior relationship, nor are they events of personal significance within the meaning of Section 2635.304(b). However, subordinates may take up a collection and employees may contribute $3 each to buy refreshments to be consumed by everyone in the immediate office to mark either such occasion.

Example 4: Subordinates may each contribute a nominal amount to a fund to give a gift to an official superior upon the occasion of that superior's transfer or promotion to a position outside the organization.

Example 5: An Assistant Secretary at the Department of the Interior is getting married. His secretary has decided that a microwave oven would be a nice gift from his staff and has informed each of the Assistant Secretary's subordinates that they should contribute $5 for the gift. Her method of collection is improper. Although she may recommend a $5 contribution, the recommendation must be coupled with a statement that the employee whose contribution is solicited is free to contribute less or nothing at all.

### SUBPART E - Impartiality in Performing Official Duties

### Section 2635.501 Overview.

(a) This subpart contains two provisions intended to ensure that an employee takes appropriate steps to avoid an appearance of loss of impartiality in the performance of his official duties. Under Section 2635.502, unless he receives prior authorization, an employee should not participate in a particular matter involving specific parties which he knows is likely to affect the financial interests of a member of his household, or in which he knows a person with whom he has a covered relationship is or represents a party, if he determines that a reasonable person with knowledge of the relevant facts would question his impartiality in the matter. An employee who is concerned that other circumstances would raise a question regarding his impartiality should use the process described in Section 2635.502 to determine whether he should or should not participate in a particular matter.

(b) Under Section 2635.503, an employee who has received an extraordinary severance or other payment from a former employer prior to entering Government service is subject, in the absence of a waiver, to a two-year period of disqualification from participation in particular matters in which that former employer is or represents a party.

**Note**: Questions regarding impartiality necessarily arise when an employee's official duties impact upon the employee's own financial interests or those of certain other persons, such as the employee's spouse or minor child. An employee is prohibited by criminal statute, 18 U.S.C. 208(a), from participating personally and substantially in an official capacity in any particular matter in which, to his knowledge, he, his spouse, general partner or minor child has a financial interest, if the particular matter will have a direct and predictable effect on that interest. The statutory prohibition also extends to an employee's participation in a particular matter in which, to his knowledge, an organization in which the employee is serving as officer, director, trustee, general partner or employee, or with whom he is negotiating or has an arrangement concerning prospective employment has a financial interest. Where the employee's participation in a particular matter would affect any one of these financial interests, the standards set forth in subparts D or F of this part apply and only a statutory waiver or exemption, as described in Sections 2635.402(d) and 2635.605(a), will enable the employee to participate in that matter. The authorization procedures in Section 2635.502(d) may not be used to authorize an employee's participation in any such matter. Where the employee complies with all terms of the waiver, the granting of a statutory waiver will be deemed to constitute a determination that the interest of the Government in the employee's participation outweighs the concern that a reasonable person may question the integrity of agency programs and operations. Similarly, where the employee meets all prerequisites for the application of one of the exemptions set forth in subpart B of part 2640 of this chapter, that also constitutes a determination that the interest of the Government in the employee's participation outweighs the concern that a reasonable person may question the integrity of agency programs and operations.

### GUIDELINES AND COMMENTARY

## 1. *What Factors Need Consideration When Offered a Gift?*

While it is not necessarily proper to accept a gift simply because its donor has a pure motive, if the purpose is improper, the benefit should invariably be refused, firmly and unequivocally, regardless of the private intent of the government official. A public employee who is considering accepting a lawful gratuity should carefully, realistically and objectively evaluate the likely motive of the person offering it. Why am I being offered this gift or favor? Would I be offered the benefit if I did not wield public influence? Who is paying for it? Is it likely to be written off as a business expense? If I accept the benefit will reasonable outsiders think that the donor has some hold on me or that I owe something in return? Since there is no offsetting public good to justify the appearance of impropriety created by the acceptance of gratuities, all close cases should be resolved against any action which raises reasonable suspicions regarding the integrity of the public employee or government in general.

## 2. *But What If I Know My Personal Decisions Will Not Affected By a Gift or Benefit?*

Some public officials take personal offense at the implication that they would allow their integrity to be compromised by a gift or favor. Most feel immune to the temptations and unconscious tendencies to give something in return, whether out of natural gratitude or the desire to encourage further gifts. "My decisions can't be influenced by a free lunch" is a common refrain from those who resent rules and ethical standards requiring rejection of gratuities and favors, especially those who view such gratuities as innocent and proper perks of public office.

These reactions unduly personalize the ethical theory and sound public policy which seek to insulate public officials from the corrupting influences of gratuities. In spite of the confidence of public employees who accept gratuities that their judgment remains unimpeded, the people who provide gratuities and favors seem to believe that it is to their advantage to do so. Often the cost is viewed as a "business" expense.

## 3. *What If Gifts Are Given After an Act?*

Gifts and favors given after an official action raise special and subtle ethical problems. Although the recipient may not have anticipated the gift and, therefore, could not have been influenced by its prospect, it may well appear to a reasonable outsider as a payment for services rendered. Such gifts also create future expectations that positive actions will be rewarded. In all but the most exceptional cases, such gifts ought to be returned with a polite but firm message that the gesture was unnecessary and could be construed as improper. If this is not feasible, they ought to be given to charity or otherwise handled in a way which makes it clear that the public employee has not accepted and does not want any personal benefit for official actions.

# II
# RECUSAL AND DISQUALIFICATION

*STANDARD*

Public employees should not take any public action under circumstances where, due to a conflict in interests, they are not certain that they can do so fairly and objectively. There are two reasons why there will not be ensured objectivity and fairness:

1. *Unavoidable Conflicts — What Do I Do?*
2. *Doubts — When Conflicts of Interest Are Involved*

*GUIDELINES AND COMMENTARY*

### 1. *Why Would Conflicts Be Unavoidable and What Do I Do?*

In some cases, conflicts caused by business, occupational or social relationships are unavoidable. In these situations, public employees and the entities they serve have independent ethical obligations to safeguard the integrity and image of the decision making process. Thus, the ethical sensitivity of the public employee should be reinforced by clear and reasonable rules requiring disclosure and, in some cases voluntary recusal (withdrawal) or involuntary disqualification.

### 2. *What if I Am Having Doubts Due to Conflicts of Interest?*

Since close cases inevitably will create at least the appearance of impropriety, doubts should be resolved in favor of disqualification or voluntary recusal.

---

### OGE RULES:

**Section 2635.402  Disqualifying financial interests.**

(a) **Statutory prohibition**.

An employee is prohibited by criminal statute, 18 U.S.C. 208(a), from participating personally and substantially in an official capacity in any particular matter in which, to his knowledge, he or any person whose interests are imputed to

---

him under this statute has a financial interest, if the particular matter will have a direct and predictable effect on that interest.

**Note**: Standards applicable when seeking non-Federal employment are contained in subpart F of this part and, if followed, will ensure that an employee does not violate 18 U.S.C. 208(a) or this section when he is negotiating for or has an arrangement concerning future employment. In all other cases where the employee's participation would violate 18 U.S.C. 208(a), an employee shall disqualify himself from participation in the matter in accordance with paragraph (c) of this section or obtain a waiver or determine that an exemption applies, as described in paragraph (d) of this section.

(b) **Definitions**.

For purposes of this section, the following definitions shall apply:

(1) **Direct and predictable effect**.

(i) A particular matter will have a direct effect on a financial interest if there is a close causal link between any decision or action to be taken in the matter and any expected effect of the matter on the financial interest. An effect may be direct even though it does not occur immediately. A particular matter will not have a direct effect on a financial interest, however, if the chain of causation is attenuated or is contingent upon the occurrence of events that are speculative or that are independent of, and unrelated to, the matter. A particular matter that has an effect on a financial interest only as a consequence of its effects on the general economy does not have a direct effect within the meaning of this subpart.

(ii) A particular matter will have a predictable effect if there is a real, as opposed to a speculative possibility that the matter will affect the financial interest. It is not necessary, however, that the magnitude of the gain or loss be known, and the dollar amount of the gain or loss is immaterial.

**Note**: If a particular matter involves a specific party or parties, generally the matter will at most only have a direct and predictable effect, for purposes of this subpart, on a financial interest of the employee in or with a party, such as the employee's interest by virtue of owning stock. There may, however, be some situations in which, under the above standards, a particular matter will have a direct and predictable effect on an employee's financial interests in or with a nonparty. For example, if a party is a corporation, a particular matter may also have a direct and predictable effect on an employee's financial interests through ownership of stock in an affiliate, parent, or subsidiary of that party. Similarly, the disposition of a protest against the award of a contract to a particular company may also have a direct and predictable effect on an employee's financial interest in another company listed as a subcontractor in the proposal of one of the competing offerors.

Example 1: An employee of the National Library of Medicine at the National Institutes of Health has just been asked to serve on the technical evaluation panel to review proposals for a new library computer search system. DEF Computer Corporation, a closely held company in which he and his wife own a majority of the stock, has submitted a proposal. Because award of the systems contract to DEF or to any other offeror will have a direct and predictable effect on both his and his wife's financial interests, the employee cannot participate on the technical evaluation team unless his disqualification has been waived.

Example 2: Upon assignment to the technical evaluation panel, the employee in the preceding example finds that DEF Computer Corporation has not submitted a proposal. Rather, LMN Corp., with which DEF competes for private sector business, is one of the six offerors. The employee is not disqualified from serving on the technical evaluation panel. Any effect on the employee's financial interests as a result of the agency's decision to award or not award the systems contract to LMN would be at most indirect and speculative.

(2) **Imputed interests**. For purposes of 18 U.S.C. 208(a) and this subpart, the financial interests of the following persons will serve to disqualify an employee to the same extent as if they were the employee's own interests:

(i) The employee's spouse;

(ii) The employee's minor child;

(iii) The employee's general partner;

(iv) An organization or entity which the employee serves as officer, director, trustee, general partner or employee; and

(v) A person with whom the employee is negotiating for or has an arrangement concerning prospective employment. (Employees who are seeking other employment should refer to and comply with the standards in subpart F of this part).

Example 1: An employee of the Department of Education serves without compensation on the board of directors of Kinder World, Inc., a nonprofit corporation that engages in good works. Even though her personal financial interests will not be affected, the employee must disqualify herself from participating in the review of a grant application submitted by Kinder World. Award or denial of the grant will affect the financial interests of Kinder World and its financial interests are imputed to her as a member of its board of directors.

Example 2: The spouse of an employee of the Food and Drug Administration has obtained a position with a well established biomedical research company. The company has developed an artificial limb for which it is seeking FDA approval and the employee would ordinarily be asked to participate in the FDA's review and approval process. The spouse is a salaried employee of the company and has no direct ownership interest in the company. Nor does she have an indirect ownership interest, as would be the case, for example, if she were participating in a pension plan that held stock in the company. Her position with the company is such that the granting or withholding of FDA approval will not have a direct and predictable effect on her salary or on her continued employment with the company. Since the FDA approval process will not affect his spouse's financial interests, the employee is not disqualified under Section 2635.402 from participating in that process. Nevertheless, the financial interests of the spouse's employer may be disqualifying under the impartiality principle, as implemented at Section 2635.502.

(3) **Particular matter**. The term particular matter encompasses only matters that involve deliberation, decision, or action that is focused upon the interests of specific persons, or a discrete and identifiable class of persons. Such a matter is covered by this subpart even if it does not involve formal parties and may include governmental action such as legislation or policy-making that is narrowly focused on the interests of such a discrete and identifiable class of persons. The term particular matter, however, does not extend to the consideration or adoption of broad policy options that are directed to the interests of a large and diverse group of persons. The particular matters covered by this subpart include a judicial or other proceeding, application, request for a ruling or other determination, contract, claim, controversy, charge, accusation or arrest.

Example 1: The Internal Revenue Service's amendment of its regulations to change the manner in which depreciation is calculated is not a particular matter, nor is the Social Security Administration's consideration of changes to its appeal procedures for disability claimants.

Example 2: Consideration by the Interstate Commerce Commission of regulations establishing safety standards for trucks on interstate highways involves a particular matter.

(4) **Personal and substantial**. To participate personally means to participate directly. It includes the direct and active supervision of the participation of a subordinate in the matter. To participate substantially means that the employee's involvement is of significance to the matter. Participation may be substantial even though it is not determinative of the outcome of a particular matter. However, it requires more than official responsibility, knowledge, perfunctory involvement, or involvement on an administrative or peripheral issue. A finding of substantiality should be based not only on the effort devoted to a matter, but also on the importance of the effort. While a series of peripheral involvements may be insubstantial, the single act of approving or participating in a critical step may be substantial.

Personal and substantial participation may occur when, for example, an employee participates through decision, approval, disapproval, recommendation, investigation or the rendering of advice in a particular matter.

(c) **Disqualification**.

Unless the employee is authorized to participate in the particular matter by virtue of a waiver or exemption described in paragraph (d) of this section or because the interest has been divested in accordance with paragraph (e) of this section, an employee shall disqualify himself from participating in a particular matter in which, to his knowledge, he or a person whose interests are imputed to him has a financial interest, if the particular matter will have a direct and predictable effect on that interest. Disqualification is accomplished by not participating in the particular matter.

(1) **Notification**. An employee who becomes aware of the need to disqualify himself from participation in a particular matter to which he has been assigned should notify the person responsible for his assignment. An employee who is responsible for his own assignment should take whatever steps are necessary to ensure that he does not participate in the matter from which he is disqualified. Appropriate oral or written notification of the employee's disqualification may be made to coworkers by the employee or a supervisor to ensure that the employee is not involved in a matter from which he is disqualified.

(2) **Documentation**.

An employee need not file a written disqualification statement unless he is required by part 2634 of this chapter to file written evidence of compliance with an ethics agreement with the Office of Government Ethics or is asked by an agency ethics official or the person responsible for his assignment to file a written disqualification statement. However, an employee may elect to create a record of his actions by providing written notice to a supervisor or other appropriate official.

Example 1: An Assistant Secretary of the Department of the Interior owns recreational property that borders on land which is being considered for annexation to a national park. Annexation would directly and predictably increase the value of her vacation property and, thus, she is disqualified from participating in any way in the Department's deliberations or decisions regarding the annexation. Because she is responsible for determining which matters she will work on, she may accomplish her disqualification merely by ensuring that she does not participate in the matter. Because of the level of her position, however, the Assistant Secretary might be wise to establish a record that she has acted properly by providing a written disqualification statement to an official superior and by providing written notification of the disqualification to subordinates to ensure that they do not raise or discuss with her any issues related to the annexation.

(d) **Waiver of or exemptions from disqualification**.

An employee who would otherwise be disqualified by 18 U.S.C. 208(a) may be permitted to participate in a particular matter where the otherwise disqualifying financial interest is the subject of a regulatory exemption or individual waiver described in this paragraph, or results from certain Indian birthrights as described in 18 U.S.C. 208(b)(4).

(1) **Regulatory exemptions**. Under 18 U.S.C. 208(b)(2), regulatory exemptions of general applicability have been issued by the Office of Government Ethics, based on its determination that particular interests are too remote or too inconsequential to affect the integrity of the services of employees to whom those exemptions apply. See the regulations in subpart B of part 2640 of this chapter, which supersede any preexisting agency regulatory exemptions.

(2) **Individual waivers**. An individual waiver enabling the employee to participate in one or more particular matters may be issued under 18 U.S.C. 208(b)(1) if, in advance of the employee's participation:

(i) The employee:

(A) Advises the Government official responsible for the employee's appointment (or other Government official to whom authority to issue such a waiver for the employee has been delegated) about the nature and circumstances of the particular matter or matters; and

(B) Makes full disclosure to such official of the nature and extent of the disqualifying financial interest; and

(ii) Such official determines, in writing, that the employee's financial interest in the particular matter or matters is not so substantial as to be deemed likely to affect the integrity of the services which the Government may expect from such employee. See also subpart C of part 2640 of this chapter, for additional guidance.

(3) Federal advisory committee member waivers. An individual waiver may be issued under 18 U.S.C. 208(b)(3) to a special Government employee serving on, or under consideration for appointment to, an advisory committee within the meaning of the Federal Advisory Committee Act if the Government official responsible for the employee's appointment (or other Government official to whom authority to issue such a waiver for the employee has been delegated):

(i) Reviews the financial disclosure report filed by the special Government employee pursuant to the Ethics in Government Act of 1978; and

(ii) Certifies in writing that the need for the individual's services outweighs the potential for a conflict of interest created by the otherwise disqualifying financial interest. See also subpart C of part 2640 of this chapter, for additional guidance.

(4) Consultation and notification regarding waivers. When practicable, an official is required to consult formally or informally with the Office of Government Ethics prior to granting a waiver referred to in paragraph (d) (2) or (3) of this section. A copy of each such waiver is to be forwarded to the Director of the Office of Government Ethics.

(e) **Divestiture of a disqualifying financial interest**.

Upon sale or other divestiture of the asset or other interest that causes his disqualification from participation in a particular matter, 18 U.S.C. 208(a) and paragraph (c) of this section will no longer prohibit the employee's participation in the matter.

(1) Voluntary divestiture. An employee who would otherwise be disqualified from participation in a particular matter may voluntarily sell or otherwise divest himself of the interest that causes the disqualification.

(2) Directed divestiture. An employee may be required to sell or otherwise divest himself of the disqualifying financial interest if his continued holding of that interest is prohibited by statute or by agency supplemental regulation issued in accordance with Section 2635.403(a), or if the agency determines in accordance with Section 2635.403(b) that a substantial conflict exists between the financial interest and the employee's duties or accomplishment of the agency's mission.

(3) Eligibility for special tax treatment. An employee who is directed to divest an interest may be eligible to defer the tax consequences of divestiture under subpart J of part 2634 of this chapter. An employee who divests before obtaining a certificate of divestiture will not be eligible for this special tax treatment.

(f) **Official duties that give rise to potential conflicts**.

Where an employee's official duties create a substantial likelihood that the employee may be assigned to a particular matter from which he is disqualified, the employee should advise his supervisor or other person responsible for his assignments of that potential so that conflicting assignments can be avoided, consistent with the agency's needs.

**Section 2635.501(b)** Under Section 2635.503, an employee who has received an extraordinary severance or other payment from a former employer prior to entering Government service is subject, in the absence of a waiver, to a two-year period of disqualification from participation in particular matters in which that former employer is or represents a party.

**Note**: Questions regarding impartiality necessarily arise when an employee's official duties impact upon the employee's own financial interests or those of certain other persons, such as the employee's spouse or minor child. An employee is prohibited by criminal statute, 18 U.S.C. 208(a), from participating personally and substantially in an official capacity in any particular matter in which, to his knowledge, he, his spouse, general partner or minor child has a financial interest, if the particular matter will have a direct and predictable effect on that interest. The statutory prohibition also extends to an employee's participation in a particular matter in which, to his knowledge, an organization in which the employee is serving as officer, director, trustee, general partner or employee, or with whom he is negotiating or has an arrangement concerning prospective employment has a financial interest. Where the employee's participation in a particular matter would affect any one of these financial interests, the standards set forth in subparts D or F of this part apply and only a statutory waiver or exemption, as described in Sections 2635.402(d) and 2635.605(a), will enable the employee to participate in that matter. The authorization procedures in Section 2635.502(d) may not be used to authorize an employee's participation in any such matter. Where the employee complies with all terms of the waiver, the granting of a statutory waiver will be deemed to constitute a determination that the interest of the Government in the employee's participation outweighs the concern that a reasonable person may question the integrity of agency programs and operations. Similarly, where the employee meets all prerequisites for the application of one of the exemptions set forth in subpart B of part 2640 of this chapter, that also constitutes a determination that the interest of the Government in the employee's participation outweighs the concern that a reasonable person may question the integrity of agency programs and operations.

**Section 2635.502 Personal and business relationships**.

(a) **Consideration of appearances by the employee**.

Where an employee knows that a particular matter involving specific parties is likely to have a direct and predictable effect on the financial interest of a member of his household, or knows that a person with whom he has a covered relationship is or represents a party to such matter, and where the employee determines that the circumstances would cause a reasonable person with knowledge of the relevant facts to question his impartiality in the matter, the employee should not participate in the matter unless he has informed the agency designee of the appearance problem and received authorization from the agency designee in accordance with paragraph (d) of this section.

(1) In considering whether a relationship would cause a reasonable person to question his impartiality, an employee may seek the assistance of his supervisor, an agency ethics official or the agency designee.

(2) An employee who is concerned that circumstances other than those specifically described in this section would raise a question regarding his impartiality should use the process described in this section to determine whether he should or should not participate in a particular matter.

(b) **Definitions**.

For purposes of this section:

(1) An employee has a covered relationship with:

(i) A person, other than a prospective employer described in Section 2635.603(c), with whom the employee has or seeks a business, contractual or other financial relationship that involves other than a routine consumer transaction; Note: An employee who is seeking employment within the meaning of Section 2635.603 shall comply with subpart F of this part rather than with this section.

(ii) A person who is a member of the employee's household, or who is a relative with whom the employee has a close personal relationship;

(iii) A person for whom the employee's spouse, parent or dependent child is, to the employee's knowledge, serving or seeking to serve as an officer, director, trustee, general partner, agent, attorney, consultant, contractor or employee;

(iv) Any person for whom the employee has, within the last year, served as officer, director, trustee, general partner, agent, attorney, consultant, contractor or employee; or

(v) An organization, other than a political party described in 26 U.S.C. 527(e), in which the employee is an active participant. Participation is active if, for example, it involves service as an official of the organization or in a capacity similar to that of a committee or subcommittee chairperson or spokesperson, or participation in directing the activities of the organization. In other cases, significant time devoted to promoting specific programs of the organization, including coordination of fundraising efforts, is an indication of active participation. Payment of dues or the donation or solicitation of financial support does not, in itself, constitute active participation.

**Note**: Nothing in this section shall be construed to suggest that an employee should not participate in a matter because of his political, religious or moral views.

(2) Direct and predictable effect has the meaning set forth in Section 2635.402(b) (1).

(3) Particular matter involving specific parties has the meaning set forth in Section 2637.102(a)(7) of this chapter.

Example 1: An employee of the General Services Administration has made an offer to purchase a restaurant owned by a local developer. The developer has submitted an offer in response to a GSA solicitation for lease of office space. Under the circumstances, she would be correct in concluding that a reasonable person would be likely to question her impartiality if she were to participate in evaluating that developer's or its competitor's lease proposal.

Example 2: An employee of the Department of Labor is providing technical assistance in drafting occupational safety and health legislation that will affect all employers of five or more persons. His wife is employed as an administrative assistant by a large corporation that will incur additional costs if the proposed legislation is enacted. Because the legislation is not a particular matter involving specific parties, the employee may continue to work on the legislation and need not be concerned that his wife's employment with an affected corporation would raise a question concerning his impartiality.

Example 3: An employee of the Defense Logistics Agency who has responsibilities for testing avionics being produced by an Air Force contractor has just learned that his sister-in-law has accepted employment as an engineer with the contractor's parent corporation. Where the parent corporation is a conglomerate, the employee could reasonably conclude that, under the circumstances, a reasonable person would not be likely to question his impartiality if he were to continue to perform his test and evaluation responsibilities.

Example 4: An engineer has just resigned from her position as vice president of an electronics company in order to accept employment with the Federal Aviation Administration in a position involving procurement responsibilities. Although the employee did not receive an extraordinary payment in connection with her resignation and has severed all financial ties with the firm, under the circumstances she would be correct in concluding that her former service as an officer of the company would be likely to cause a reasonable person to question her impartiality if she were to participate in the administration of a DOT contract for which the firm is a first-tier subcontractor.

Example 5: An employee of the Internal Revenue Service is a member of a private organization whose purpose is to restore a Victorian- era railroad station and she chairs its annual fundraising drive. Under the circumstances, the employee would be correct in concluding that her active membership in the organization would be likely to cause a reasonable person to question her impartiality if she were to participate in an IRS determination regarding the tax- exempt status of the organization.

(c) **Determination by agency designee**.

Where he has information concerning a potential appearance problem arising from the financial interest of a member of the employee's household in a particular matter involving specific parties, or from the role in such matter of a person with whom the employee has a covered relationship, the agency designee may make an independent determination as to whether a reasonable person with knowledge of the relevant facts would be likely to question the employee's impartiality in the matter. Ordinarily, the agency designee's determination will be initiated by information provided by the employee pursuant to paragraph (a) of this section. However, at any time, including after the employee has disqualified himself from participation in a matter pursuant to paragraph (e) of this section, the agency designee may make this determination on his own initiative or when requested by the employee's supervisor or any other person responsible for the employee's assignment.

(1) If the agency designee determines that the employee's impartiality is likely to be questioned, he shall then determine, in accordance with paragraph (d) of this section, whether the employee should be authorized to participate in the matter. Where the agency designee determines that the employee's participation should not be authorized, the employee will be disqualified from participation in the matter in accordance with paragraph (e) of this section.

(2) If the agency designee determines that the employee's impartiality is not likely to be questioned, he may advise the employee, including an employee who has reached a contrary conclusion under paragraph (a) of this section, that the employee's participation in the matter would be proper.

(d) **Authorization by agency designee**.

Where an employee's participation in a particular matter involving specific parties would not violate 18 U.S.C. 208(a), but would raise a question in the mind of a reasonable person about his impartiality, the agency designee may authorize the employee to participate in the matter based on a determination, made in light of all relevant circumstances, that the interest of the Government in the employee's participation outweighs the concern that a reasonable person may question the integrity of the agency's programs and operations. Factors which may be taken into consideration include:

(1) The nature of the relationship involved;

(2) The effect that resolution of the matter would have upon the financial interests of the person involved in the relationship;

(3) The nature and importance of the employee's role in the matter, including the extent to which the employee is called upon to exercise discretion in the matter;

(4) The sensitivity of the matter;

(5) The difficulty of reassigning the matter to another employee; and

(6) Adjustments that may be made in the employee's duties that would reduce or eliminate the likelihood that a reasonable person would question the employee's impartiality.

Authorization by the agency designee shall be documented in writing at the agency designee's discretion or when requested by the employee. An employee who has been authorized to participate in a particular matter involving specific parties may not thereafter disqualify himself from participation in the matter on the basis of an appearance problem involving the same circumstances that have been considered by the agency designee.

Example 1: The Deputy Director of Personnel for the Department of the Treasury and an attorney with the Department's Office of General Counsel are general partners in a real estate partnership. The Deputy Director advises his supervisor, the Director of Personnel, of the relationship upon being assigned to a selection panel for a position for which his partner has applied. If selected, the partner would receive a substantial increase in salary. The agency designee cannot authorize the Deputy Director to participate on the panel under the authority of this section since the Deputy Director is prohibited by criminal statute, 18 U.S.C. 208(a), from participating in a particular matter affecting the financial interest of a person who is his general partner. See Section 2635.402.

Example 2: A new employee of the Securities and Exchange Commission is assigned to an investigation of insider trading by the brokerage house where she had recently been employed. Because of the sensitivity of the investigation, the agency designee may be unable to conclude that the Government's interest in the employee's participation in the investigation outweighs the concern that a reasonable person may question the integrity of the investigation, even though the employee has severed all financial ties with the company. Based on consideration of all relevant circumstances, the agency designee might determine, however, that it is in the interest of the Government for the employee to pass on a routine filing by the particular brokerage house.

Example 3: An Internal Revenue Service employee involved in a long and complex tax audit is advised by her son that he has just accepted an entry- level management position with a corporation whose taxes are the subject of the audit. Because the audit is essentially complete and because the employee is the only one with an intimate knowledge of the case, the agency designee might determine, after considering all relevant circumstances, that it is in the Government's interest for the employee to complete the audit, which is subject to additional levels of review.

(e) **Disqualification.**

Unless the employee is authorized to participate in the matter under paragraph (d) of this section, an employee shall not participate in a particular matter involving specific parties when he or the agency designee has concluded, in accordance with paragraph (a) or (c) of this section, that the financial interest of a member of the employee's household, or the role of a person with whom he has a covered relationship, is likely to raise a question in the mind of a reasonable person about his impartiality. Disqualification is accomplished by not participating in the matter.

(1) **Notification.** An employee who becomes aware of the need to disqualify himself from participation in a particular matter involving specific parties to which he has been assigned should notify the person responsible for his assignment. An employee who is responsible for his own assignment should take whatever steps are necessary to ensure that he does not participate in the matter from which he is disqualified. Appropriate oral or written notification of the employee's disqualification may be made to coworkers by the employee or a supervisor to ensure that the employee is not involved in a particular matter involving specific parties from which he is disqualified.

(2) **Documentation.** An employee need not file a written disqualification statement unless he is required by part 2634 of this chapter to file written evidence of compliance with an ethics agreement with the Office of Government Ethics or is specifically asked by an agency ethics official or the person responsible for his assignment to file a written disqualification

statement. However, an employee may elect to create a record of his actions by providing written notice to a supervisor or other appropriate official.

(f) **Relevant considerations**. An employee's reputation for honesty and integrity is not a relevant consideration for purposes of any determination required by this section.

**Section 2635.503 Extraordinary payments from former employers**.

(a) **Disqualification requirement**.

Except as provided in paragraph (c) of this section, an employee shall be disqualified for two years from participating in any particular matter in which a former employer is a party or represents a party if he received an extraordinary payment from that person prior to entering Government service. The two-year period of disqualification begins to run on the date that the extraordinary payment is received.

Example 1: Following his confirmation hearings and one month before his scheduled swearing in, a nominee to the position of Assistant Secretary of a department received an extraordinary payment from his employer. For one year and 11 months after his swearing in, the Assistant Secretary may not participate in any particular matter to which his former employer is a party.

Example 2: An employee received an extraordinary payment from her former employer, a coal mine operator, prior to entering on duty with the Department of the Interior. For two years thereafter, she may not participate in a determination regarding her former employer's obligation to reclaim a particular mining site, because her former employer is a party to the matter. However, she may help to draft reclamation legislation affecting all coal mining operations because this legislation does not involve any parties.

(b) **Definitions**.

For purposes of this section, the following definitions shall apply:

(1) Extraordinary payment means any item, including cash or an investment interest, with a value in excess of $10,000, which is paid:

(i) On the basis of a determination made after it became known to the former employer that the individual was being considered for or had accepted a Government position; and

(ii) Other than pursuant to the former employer's established compensation, partnership, or benefits program. A compensation, partnership, or benefits program will be deemed an established program if it is contained in bylaws, a contract or other written form, or if there is a history of similar payments made to others not entering into Federal service.

Example 1: The vice president of a small corporation is nominated to be an ambassador. In recognition of his service to the corporation, the board of directors votes to pay him $50,000 upon his confirmation in addition to the regular severance payment provided for by the corporate bylaws. The regular severance payment is not an extraordinary payment. The gratuitous payment of $50,000 is an extraordinary payment, since the corporation had not made similar payments to other departing officers.

(2) Former employer includes any person which the employee served as an officer, director, trustee, general partner, agent, attorney, consultant, contractor or employee.

(c) **Waiver of disqualification**.

The disqualification requirement of this section may be waived based on a finding that the amount of the payment was not so substantial as to cause a reasonable person to question the employee's ability to act impartially in a matter in which the former employer is or represents a party. The waiver shall be in writing and may be given only by the head of the agency or, where the recipient of the payment is the head of the agency, by the President or his designee. Waiver authority may be delegated by agency heads to any person who has been delegated authority to issue individual waivers under 18 U.S.C. 208(b) for the employee who is the recipient of the extraordinary payment.

## SUBPART F - Seeking Other Employment

### Section 2635.601 Overview.

This subpart contains a disqualification requirement that applies to employees when seeking employment with persons whose financial interests would be directly and predictably affected by particular matters in which the employees participate personally and substantially. Specifically, it addresses the requirement of 18 U.S.C. 208(a) that an employee disqualify himself from participation in any particular matter that will have a direct and predictable effect on the financial interests of a person "with whom he is negotiating or has any arrangement concerning prospective employment." See Section 2635.402 and Section 2640.103 of this chapter. Beyond this statutory requirement, it also addresses the issues of lack of impartiality that require disqualification from particular matters affecting the financial interests of a prospective employer when an employee's actions in seeking employment fall short of actual employment negotiations.

### Section 2635.602 Applicability and related considerations.

To ensure that he does not violate 18 U.S.C. 208(a) or the principles of ethical conduct contained in Section 2635.101(b), an employee who is seeking employment or who has an arrangement concerning prospective employment shall comply with the applicable disqualification requirements of Sections 2635.604 and 2635.606 if particular matters in which the employee will be participating personally and substantially would directly and predictably affect the financial interests of a prospective employer or of a person with whom he has an arrangement concerning prospective employment. Compliance with this subpart also will ensure that the employee does not violate subpart D or E of this part.

**Note**: An employee who is seeking employment with a person whose financial interests are not affected directly and predictably by particular matters in which he participates personally and substantially has no obligation under this subpart. An employee may, however, be subject to other statutes which impose requirements on employment contacts or discussions, such as 41 U.S.C. 423(c), applicable to agency officials involved in certain procurement matters.

(a) **Related employment restrictions**

(1) Outside employment while a Federal employee. An employee who is contemplating outside employment to be undertaken concurrently with his Federal employment must abide by any limitations applicable to his outside activities under subparts G and H of this part. He must also comply with any disqualification requirement that may be applicable under subpart D or E of this part as a result of his outside employment activities.

(2) Post-employment restrictions. An employee who is contemplating employment to be undertaken following the termination of his Federal employment should consult an agency ethics official to obtain advice regarding any post-employment restrictions that may be applicable. Regulations implementing the Governmentwide post- employment statute, 18 U.S.C. 207, are contained in parts 2637 and 2641 of this chapter. Employees are cautioned that they may be subject to additional statutory prohibitions on post-employment acceptance of compensation from contractors, such as 41 U.S.C. 423(d).

(b) **Interview trips and entertainment**.

Where a prospective employer who is a prohibited source as defined in Section 2635.203(d) offers to reimburse an employee's travel expenses, or provide other reasonable amenities incident to employment discussions, the employee may accept such amenities in accordance with Section 2635.204(e)(3).

**Section 2635.603 Definitions**.

For purposes of this subpart:

(a) Employment means any form of non-Federal employment or business relationship involving the provision of personal services by the employee, whether to be undertaken at the same time as or subsequent to Federal employment. It includes but is not limited to personal services as an officer, director, employee, agent, attorney, consultant, contractor, general partner or trustee.

Example 1: An employee of the Bureau of Indian Affairs who has announced her intention to retire is approached by tribal representatives concerning a possible consulting contract with the tribe. The independent contractual relationship the tribe wishes to negotiate is employment for purposes of this subpart.

Example 2: An employee of the Department of Health and Human Services is invited to a meeting with officials of a nonprofit corporation to discuss the possibility of his serving as a member of the corporation's board of directors. Service, with or without compensation, as a member of the board of directors constitutes employment for purposes of this subpart.

(b) An employee is seeking employment once he has begun seeking employment within the meaning of paragraph (b)(1) of this section and until he is no longer seeking employment within the meaning of paragraph (b)(2) of this section.

(1) An employee has begun seeking employment if he has directly or indirectly:

(i) Engaged in negotiations for employment with any person. For these purposes, as for 18 U.S.C. 208(a), the term negotiations means discussion or communication with another person, or such person's agent or intermediary, mutually conducted with a view toward reaching an agreement regarding possible employment with that person. The term is not limited to discussions of specific terms and conditions of employment in a specific position;

(ii) Made an unsolicited communication to any person, or such person's agent or intermediary, regarding possible employment with that person. However, the employee has not begun seeking employment if that communication was:

(A) For the sole purpose of requesting a job application; or

(B) For the purpose of submitting a resume or other employment proposal to a person affected by the performance or nonperformance of the employee's duties only as part of an industry or other discrete class. The employee will be considered to have begun seeking employment upon receipt of any response indicating an interest in employment discussions; or

(iii) Made a response other than rejection to an unsolicited communication from any person, or such person's agent or intermediary, regarding possible employment with that person.

(2) An employee is no longer seeking employment when:

(i) The employee or the prospective employer rejects the possibility of employment and all discussions of possible employment have terminated; or

(ii) Two months have transpired after the employee's dispatch of an unsolicited resume or employment proposal, provided the employee has received no indication of interest in employment discussions from the prospective employer.

(3) For purposes of this definition, a response that defers discussions until the foreseeable future does not constitute rejection of an unsolicited employment overture, proposal, or resume nor rejection of a prospective employment possibility.

Example 1: An employee of the Health Care Financing Administration is complimented on her work by an official of a State Health Department who asks her to call if she is ever interested in leaving Federal service. The employee explains to the State official that she is very happy with her job at HCFA and is not interested in another job. She thanks him for his compliment regarding her work and adds that she'll remember his interest if she ever decides to leave the Government. The employee has rejected the unsolicited employment overture and has not begun seeking employment.

Example 2: The employee in the preceding example responds by stating that she cannot discuss future employment while she is working on a project affecting the State's health care funding but would like to discuss employment with the State when the project is completed. Because the employee has merely deferred employment discussions until the foreseeable future, she has begun seeking employment with the State Health Department.

Example 3: An employee of the Defense Contract Audit

Agency is auditing the overhead accounts of an Army contractor. While at the contractor's headquarters, the head of the contractor's accounting division tells the employee that his division is thinking about hiring another accountant and asks whether the employee might be interested in leaving DCAA. The DCAA employee says he is interested in knowing what kind of work would be involved. They discuss the duties of the position the accounting division would like to fill and the DCAA employee's qualifications for the position. They do not discuss salary. The head of the division explains that he has not yet received authorization to fill the particular position and will get back to the employee when he obtains the necessary approval for additional staffing. The employee and the contractor's official have engaged in negotiations regarding possible employment. The employee has begun seeking employment with the Army contractor.

Example 4: An employee of the Occupational Safety and Health Administration helping to draft safety standards applicable to the textile industry has mailed his resume to 25 textile manufacturers. He has not begun seeking employment with any of the twenty-five. If he receives a response from one of the resume recipients indicating an interest in employment discussions, the employee will have begun seeking employment with the respondent at that time.

Example 5: A special Government employee of the Federal Deposit Insurance Corporation is serving on an advisory committee formed for the purpose of reviewing rules applicable to all member banks. She mails an unsolicited letter to a member bank offering her services as a contract consultant. She has not begun seeking employment with the bank until she receives some response indicating an interest in discussing her employment proposal. A letter merely acknowledging receipt of the proposal is not an indication of interest in employment discussions.

Example 6: A geologist employed by the U.S. Geological Survey has been working as a member of a team preparing the Government's case in an action brought by the Government against six oil companies. The geologist sends her resume to an oil company that is a named defendant in the action. The geologist has begun seeking employment with that oil company and will be seeking employment for two months from the date the resume was mailed. However, if she withdraws her application or is notified within the two-month period that her resume has been rejected, she will no longer be seeking employment with the oil company as of the date she makes such withdrawal or receives such notification.

(c) Prospective employer means any person with whom the employee is seeking employment. Where contacts that constitute seeking employment are made by or with an agent or other intermediary, the term prospective employer includes:

(1) A person who uses that agent or other intermediary for the purpose of seeking to establish an employment relationship with the employee if the agent identifies the prospective employer to the employee; and

(2) A person contacted by the employee's agent or other intermediary for the purpose of seeking to establish an employment relationship if the agent identifies the prospective employer to the employee.

Example 1: An employee of the Federal Aviation Administration has overall responsibility for airport safety inspections in a three- state area. She has retained an employment search firm to help her find another job. The search firm has just reported to the FAA employee that it has given her resume to and had promising discussions with two airport authorities within her jurisdiction. Even though the employee has not personally had employment discussions with either, each airport authority is her prospective employer. She began seeking employment with each upon learning its identity and that it has been given her resume.

(d) Direct and predictable effect, particular matter, and personal and substantial have the respective meanings set forth in Section 2635.402(b)(1), (3) and (4).

**Section 2635.604 Disqualification while seeking employment.**

(a) **Obligation to disqualify**. Unless the employee's participation is authorized in accordance with Section

2635.605, the employee shall not participate personally and substantially in a particular matter that, to his knowledge, has a direct and predictable effect on the financial interests of a prospective employer with whom he is seeking employment within the meaning of Section 2635.603(b). Disqualification is accomplished by not participating in the particular matter.

(b) **Notification**. An employee who becomes aware of the need to disqualify himself from participation in a particular matter to which he has been assigned should notify the person responsible for his assignment. An employee who is responsible for his own assignment should take whatever steps are necessary to ensure that he does not participate personally and substantially in the matter from which he is disqualified. Appropriate oral or written notification of the employee's disqualification may be made to coworkers by the employee or a supervisor to ensure that the employee is not involved in a matter from which he is disqualified.

(c) **Documentation**. An employee need not file a written disqualification statement unless he is required by part 2634 of this chapter to file written evidence of compliance with an ethics agreement with the Office of Government Ethics or is specifically asked by an agency ethics official or the person responsible for his assignment to file a written disqualification statement. However, an employee may elect to create a record of his actions by providing written notice to a supervisor or other appropriate official.

Example 1: An employee of the Department of Veterans Affairs is participating in the audit of a contract for laboratory support services. Before sending his resume to a lab which is a subcontractor under the VA contract, the employee should disqualify himself from participation in the audit. Since he cannot withdraw from participation in the contract audit without the approval of his supervisor, he should disclose his intentions to his supervisor in order that appropriate adjustments in his work assignments can be made.

Example 2: An employee of the Food and Drug Administration is contacted in writing by a pharmaceutical company concerning possible employment with the company. The employee is involved in testing a drug for which the company is seeking FDA approval. Before making a response that is not a rejection, the employee should disqualify himself from further participation in the testing. Where he has authority to ask his colleague to assume his testing responsibilities, he may accomplish his disqualification by transferring the work to that coworker. However, to ensure that his colleague and others with whom he had been working on the recommendations do not seek his advice regarding testing or otherwise involve him in the matter, it may be necessary for him to advise those individuals of his disqualification.

Example 3: The General Counsel of a regulatory agency wishes to engage in discussions regarding possible employment as corporate counsel of a regulated entity. Matters directly affecting the financial interests of the regulated entity are pending within the Office of General Counsel, but the General Counsel will not be called upon to act in any such matter because signature authority for that particular class of matters has been delegated to an Assistant General Counsel. Because the General Counsel is responsible for assigning work within the Office of General Counsel, he can in fact accomplish his disqualification by simply avoiding any involvement in matters affecting the regulated entity. However, because it is likely to be assumed by others that the General Counsel is involved in all matters within the cognizance of the Office of General Counsel, he would be wise to file a written disqualification statement with the Commissioners of the regulatory agency and provide his subordinates with written notification of his disqualification, or he may be specifically asked by an agency ethics official or the Commissioners to file a written disqualification statement.

Example 4: A scientist is employed by the National Science Foundation as a special Government employee to serve on a panel that reviews grant applications to fund research relating to deterioration of the ozone layer. She is discussing possible employment as a member of the faculty of a university that several years earlier received an NSF grant to study the effect of fluorocarbons, but has no grant application pending. As long as the university does not submit a new application for the panel's review, the employee would not have to take any action to effect disqualification.

(d) **Agency determination of substantial conflict**. Where the agency determines that the employee's action in seeking employment with a particular person will require his disqualification from matters so central or critical to the performance of his official duties that the employee's ability to perform the duties of his position would be materially impaired, the agency may allow the employee to take annual leave or leave without pay while seeking employment, or may take other appropriate administrative action.

**Section 2635.605 Waiver or authorization permitting participation while seeking employment.**

(a) **Waiver.**

Where, as defined in Section 2635.603(b)(1)(i), an employee is engaged in discussions that constitute employment negotiations for purposes of 18 U.S.C. 208(a), the employee may participate personally and substantially in a particular matter that has a direct and predictable effect on the financial interests of a prospective employer only after receiving a written waiver issued under the authority of 18 U.S.C. 208(b)(1) or (b)(3). These waivers are described in Section 2635.402(d). See also subpart C of part 2640 of this chapter. For certain employees, a regulatory exemption under the authority of 18 U.S.C. 208(b)(2) may also apply (see subpart B of part 2640 of this chapter).

Example 1: An employee of the Department of Agriculture has had two telephone conversations with an orange grower regarding possible employment. They have discussed the employee's qualifications for a particular position with the grower, but have not yet discussed salary or other specific terms of employment. The employee is negotiating for employment within the meaning of 18 U.S.C. 208(a) and Section 2635.603(b)(1) (i). In the absence of a written waiver issued under 18 U.S.C. 208(b) (1), she may not take official action on a complaint filed by a competitor alleging that the grower has shipped oranges in violation of applicable quotas.

(b) **Authorization by agency designee.**

Where an employee is seeking employment within the meaning of Section 2635.603(b)(1)(ii) or (iii), a reasonable person would be likely to question his impartiality if he were to participate personally and substantially in a particular matter that has a direct and predictable effect on the financial interests of any such prospective employer. The employee may participate in such matters only where the agency designee has authorized his participation in accordance with the standards set forth in Section 2635.502(d).

Example 1: Within the past month, an employee of the Education Department mailed her resume to a university. She is thus seeking employment with the university within the meaning of Section 2635.603(b)(1) (ii) even though she has received no reply. In the absence of specific authorization by the agency designee in accordance with Section 2635.502(d), she may not participate in an assignment to review a grant application submitted by the university.

**Section 2635.606 Disqualification based on an arrangement concerning prospective employment or otherwise after negotiations**.

(a) **Employment or arrangement concerning employment**.

An employee shall be disqualified from participating personally and substantially in a particular matter that has a direct and predictable effect on the financial interests of the person by whom he is employed or with whom he has an arrangement concerning future employment, unless authorized to participate in the matter by a written waiver issued under the authority of 18 U.S.C. 208 (b)(1) or (b)(3), or by a regulatory exemption under the authority of 18 U.S.C. 208(b)(2). These waivers and exemptions are described in Section 2635.402(d). See also subparts B and C of part 2640 of this chapter.

Example 1: A military officer has accepted a job with a defense contractor to begin in six months, after his retirement from military service. During the period that he remains with the Government, the officer may not participate in the administration of a contract with that particular defense contractor unless he has received a written waiver under the authority of 18 U.S.C. 208(b)(1).

Example 2: An accountant has just been offered a job with the Comptroller of the Currency which involves a two-year limited appointment. Her private employer, a large corporation, believes the job will enhance her skills and has agreed to give her a two-year unpaid leave of absence at the end of which she has agreed to return to work for the corporation. During the two-year period she is to be a COC employee, the accountant will have an arrangement concerning future employment with the corporation that will require her disqualification from participation in any particular matter that will have a direct and predictable effect on the corporation's financial interests.

(b) **Offer rejected or not made**. The agency designee for the purpose of Section 2635.502(c) may, in an appropriate case, determine that an employee not covered by the preceding paragraph who has sought but is no longer seeking employment nevertheless shall be subject to a period of disqualification upon the conclusion of employment negotiations. Any such determination shall be based on a consideration of all the relevant factors, including those listed in Section 2635.502(d), and a determination that the concern that a reasonable person may question the integrity of the agency's decision making process outweighs the Government's interest in the employee's participation in the particular matter.

Example 1: An employee of the Securities and Exchange Commission was relieved of responsibility for an investigation of a broker-dealer while seeking employment with the law firm representing the broker-dealer in that matter. The firm did not offer her the partnership position she sought. Even though she is no longer seeking employment with the firm, she may continue to be disqualified from participating in the investigation based on a determination by the agency designee that the concern that a reasonable person might question whether, in view of the history of the employment negotiations, she could act impartially in the matter outweighs the Government's interest in her participation.

# III
# BIAS AND FAVORITISM

*STANDARD*

Public employees should exercise the powers and prerogatives of office fairly and without prejudice or favoritism. It is improper to use public authority to reward relatives, friends or political supporters or to hinder or punish enemies and opponents.

---

**OGE RULES:**

Section 2635.902(gg) The prohibition against participation in the appointment or promotion of relatives (5 U.S.C. 3110).

---

*GUIDELINES AND COMMENTARY*

### *How Important Are Qualifications?*

Public employees should make all employment decisions on the merits, only choosing those who are well qualified. Subjective matters like personality, temperament and compatibility are relevant and it is not always necessary to pick the person with the highest qualifications. And, politicians employing staff to help advance political and policy goals will naturally and appropriately consider other factors — such as the level of support for those policies — as vital qualifications. These factors, however, do not diminish the fact that a responsible employment decision seeks out those who are more than barely qualified.

### *Should Ideological Views Be Disregarded?*

Though ideology and history of support are valid considerations in clearly political positions, they are inappropriate in the vast majority of government jobs. In spite of the long tradition of patronage, public jobs should not be treated as the spoils of victory.

# IV
# INTERVENING IN ADMINISTRATIVE ACTIONS

## *STANDARD*

Public officials should be extremely cautious about directly or indirectly intervening with normal decision making, investigatory or adjudicative processes of governmental bodies since such intervention can threaten the ability of government administrators to exercise independent objective judgment on the merits.

## *GUIDELINES AND COMMENTARY*

### *What Is the Importance of Preserving Independence of Administrators?*

All public employees should avoid using or appearing to use political influence in any way that is likely to cause another public employee to consider inappropriate factors in exercising public authority. Acts either intended to or likely to be construed as enticements, trade-offs, ingratiation, intimidation, or coercion are improper.

### *What Is the General Rule?*

Generally, intervention with an administrative agency is proper only if it is strictly limited to assuring fairness of the procedures and the intervener consciously avoids seeking to unduly influence the decision making process. Those who intervene should firmly, explicitly and unambiguously convey their limited purposes to reduce the possibility of direct or indirect pressure on administrators which could reasonably appear to influence the substantive decision.

# PRINCIPLE 3:
# Be Publicly Accountable

Public employees should assure that government is conducted openly, efficiently, equitably and honorably in a manner that permits the citizenry to make informed judgments and hold government officials accountable.

The following standards will be discussed in this section:


## I. OVERSIGHT

## II. OPENNESS

## III. DUTY TO IMPROVE SYSTEM

### A. Corrective Actions

### B. Supervisor's Duty

## IV. SELF-POLICING

## V. WHISTLEBLOWING AND LEAKING


# I
# OVERSIGHT

*STANDARD*

Public employees should assure that those to whom they have delegated public power, including their staffs and administrative agencies, carry out their responsibilities efficiently, equitably and ethically.

Given this standard, two issues related to implementing policy are:

1. *Auditing and Reporting Procedures*
2. *Staff Training*

*GUIDELINES AND COMMENTARY*

### 1. *Who Is Responsible for Auditing and Reporting Procedures?*

It is the duty of public employees with agency oversight responsibilities to develop effective auditing and reporting procedures which permit the exercise of vigilant oversight.

### 2. *Who Is Responsible for Ensuring Staff Training?*

Persons in supervisory positions should assure that their staff knows and understands the legal and ethical obligations applicable to their duties.

# II
# OPENNESS

*STANDARD*

Public employees should exercise the authority of their offices openly so that the public is informed about governmental decisions and the citizenry can hold them accountable for their actions.

Given this standard, three issues related to implementing policy are:

1. *Meetings*
2. *Exceptions*
3. *Evasion of Openness Rules*

*GUIDELINES AND COMMENTARY*

### 1. *What Types of Meetings Are Considered Appropriate?*

Secret or closed meetings and back room deals which conceal from the public facts that bear on its ability to exercise responsible citizenship are improper, even when made in the name of the "public good" or "national security." Public employees should be especially scrupulous about maintaining maximum openness in dealing with issues of compensation and benefits for public employees.

### 2. *Are There Exceptions?*

Although secrecy or confidentiality occasionally are in the public interest (as with police undercover and foreign intelligence operations and military plans), exceptions to the general rule of openness should be rare and the principles and procedures for determining those exceptions should be subject to scrutiny, debate and oversight.

### 3. *Can You Evade Openness Rules While Being "Legal"?*

Public employees should honor the spirit and intent of open government rules and not engage in subterfuges or legalistic schemes to avoid them. While public employees should abide by the letter and spirit of all rules, open meeting, freedom of information, and "sunshine" laws are especially important because they reinforce accountability by requiring public business to be conducted in a way that assures citizen access to political processes. Although these rules tend to be unpopular with many public employees who believe they unreasonably invade privacy and encumber government operations, it is improper to engage in tactics which evade their spirit.

# III
# DUTY TO IMPROVE SYSTEM

*STANDARD*

Public employees who believe that a law or policy is not achieving its intended purpose, is creating unintended harms, or is wasteful or inefficient, should take affirmative steps to improve procedures in a way that will increase the fairness and quality of government services and assure that policies are implemented equitably, efficiently and economically.

Given this standard, two issues related to improving the system are:

A. *Corrective Actions*
B. *Supervisor's Duty*

# III(A)
# Corrective Actions

## STANDARD

Public employees should take whatever actions they can to correct problems, streamline procedures and improve services. Where desirable changes exceed authority, public employees should promptly and forcefully recommend reform to the appropriate person or body.

## GUIDELINES AND COMMENTARY

There is a tendency in all organizations to define one's responsibilities narrowly, fostering an "it's-not-my-job" mentality with respect to defects in policy or implementation. It is every public employee's job to see that the government serves the people well by assuring that it is responsive, respectful, efficient, economical and fair.

# III(B)
# Supervisor's Duty

## STANDARD

In order to encourage a broad sense of responsibility for both the results and methods of government action, supervisors should develop a working environment that fosters constructive criticism and creative problem solving.

## GUIDELINES AND COMMENTARY

Establishing a healthy atmosphere where everyone is willing to be accountable for the end product is difficult because many government organizations are overworked and understaffed. There is a tendency to view criticisms, and even constructive suggestions for change, as more things to do or worry about which interfere with the performance of existing duties. Consequently, a negative bureaucratic culture often develops which can deter and discourage the questioning of methods and the evaluation of results. Responsible public employees should be aware of this tendency and resist unthinking bureaucratic tendencies to "kill the messenger."

# IV
# SELF-POLICING

## STANDARD

Public employees should maintain the integrity and trustworthiness of government by taking whatever steps are necessary, including reporting improper conduct to appropriate authorities, to prevent the unlawful or unethical use of public position, authority or resources.

Given this standard, four issues related to self-policing are:

1. *Principles of Public Trust and Accountability*

2. *Establishing an Ethical Atmosphere That Deters Wrongdoing*

3. *Overcoming Practical and Emotional Impediments*

4. *Establishing Mandatory Reporting of Policies*

## GUIDELINES AND COMMENTARY

### 1. *Do Public Employees Have Special Responsibilities in Dealing With Concepts of Public Trust and Accountability?*

Public employees are often in the best position to observe and take actions against unlawful and unethical uses of public position, authority and resources. In fact, many such uses could not occur without the active involvement or, at least, the acquiescence of colleagues and subordinates. The principles of public trust and accountability combine to place a special obligation on persons in public office to refuse to cooperate, to actively discourage, and if necessary to prevent improper conduct, to report violations of both law and ethical standards.

### 2. *What Is the Importance of Establishing an Ethical Atmosphere That Deters Wrongdoing?*

It is important to establish an atmosphere in government where potential wrongdoers undertake very high risk in seeking to misuse government office. This occurs when it becomes known that the pride and ethical commitment of all public employees impels them to police their own profession. The person who violates the public trust, not the one who prevents or reports such violations ought to bear the brunt of disapproval from the public and government colleagues.

### 3. *How Do You Overcome Practical and Emotional Impediments?*

Unfortunately, there are powerful practical and psychological impediments which make self-policing risky and unrewarding. On a practical level, saying no to a colleague, superior or a powerful political figure who has influence with the public employee's superiors or over the budget of a particular department can easily result in reprisals. On the emotional level, the inherent desire to be liked and an aversion to being considered a "goody two-shoes," someone who's "not on the team," or worse, a "stoolie," tends to deter active pursuit of ethical principles in contexts where the prevalent policy seems to be, "don't rock the boat," "to get along, go along." It is especially important, therefore, that those who wield power do so to encourage and protect the conscientious employee who cares about doing what is right.

### 4. *What About Establishing Mandatory Report Policies?*

In some cases, reporting structures, such as policies requiring administrators to report the nature and substance of contacts from those who seek to influence their decision making, can make it harder for those who seek to use their influence improperly and easier for those who wish to be insulated from political pressures and financial temptations. For example, administrators of state programs might be required to report and describe contacts from politicians who are intervening on behalf of constituents or friends.

# V
# WHISTLEBLOWING AND LEAKING

*STANDARD*

***Whistleblowing***: Public employees, having the "good faith" belief that the public interest requires the disclosure of governmental policies or actions thought to be unlawful or improper, should reveal their information to appropriate authorities.

---

**OGE RULE:**

**Section 2635.101(b)(11)**: Employees shall disclose waste, fraud, abuse, and corruption to appropriate authorities.

---

*GUIDELINES AND COMMENTARY*

### *What is Whistleblowing?*

Whistleblowing is most often justified when it is the only practical way to reveal illegal conduct or major abuses of public authority. The decision to blow the whistle, however, must be regarded with the utmost seriousness. Although whistleblowing can represent the highest form of loyalty to an institution and to democratic processes, it often requires breaching traditional notions of loyalty to one's colleagues and organization.

In addition, it may involve the violation of professional obligations of confidentiality. Thus, the act of whistleblowing invariably incurs hostility and resentment and tends to undermine trust and create an atmosphere of suspicion. Yet, in spite of the personal and institutional costs, *whistleblowing is sometimes essential to the public interest and morally justified as a means of preventing or correcting serious wrongs.*

### *How Should Whistleblowers Be Treated?*

Without the risk that conscientious public employees will, when necessary, disclose unlawful or improper governmental activities, the likelihood of illegal secret policies and unaccountable and arrogant decision making increases. Hence, *persons who blow the whistle in good faith act in the public interest. It is therefore improper for a public employee to harass, punish, or seek other reprisals against public employees who seek to hold government accountable through conscientious whistleblowing.*

### STANDARD

**Leaking:** Except in matters of great public importance where identifying oneself as the source of information would involve unreasonable personal risks, public employees should not secretly reveal confidential governmental matters or allege improprieties.

### When is Leaking Proper?

Although leaking is presumptively improper, there are rare circumstances where it is justified as a means of holding the government accountable for improper covert actions. Many issues of great importance (e.g., Watergate, the Pentagon Papers, illegal CIA assassination policies) came to light only because of leakers who acted in the public interest but sought to protect themselves and their families from the ramifications of their revelations. Because of general principles of trust, honor, and professional discretion, however, disclosure of confidential information or documents through secret leaking is justified only to advance a compelling public interest.

In the absence of a clear and compelling interest in disclosure, *public employees should honor their confidences and legal obligations to maintain the secrecy of specified information* (e.g., classified documents, grand jury testimony, medical or psychiatric records, reports about juvenile abuse, etc.). It is *not* proper, for example, to leak information simply to give one news organization a competitive advantage over another about matters that will be made public in due time (e.g., revealing the contents of a report a few days before it is to be formally issued). *Nor is it proper to leak information simply as a means of affording the leaker some personal or political advantage.*

### What Is the Difference Between Whistleblowing and Leaking?

While both whistleblowing and leaking may be acts of conscience, whistleblowers act overtly and hence take greater risks and subject themselves to significant personal abuse including reprisals. In contrast, leakers act covertly and are essentially unaccountable for the consequences of their actions. Since it is fairer that criticisms and charges be made on the record, *whistleblowing is preferable to leaking. In fact, in most cases, leaking is an improper violation of confidentiality and fairness.*

# PRINCIPLE 4:
# Lead With Citizenship

Public employees should honor and respect the principles and spirit of representative democracy and set a positive example of good citizenship by scrupulously observing the letter and spirit of laws and rules.

The following standards will be discussed in this section:

### I. OBEYING ALL LAWS

### II. ARTIFICES AND SCHEMES

### III. INTEGRITY OF THE PROCESS

### IV. CIVIL DISOBEDIENCE

# I
# OBEYING ALL LAWS

*STANDARD*
Public employees have a special obligation to obey all laws and regulations.

---

**OGE RULE:**

**2635.101(b)(14)** Employees shall endeavor to avoid any actions creating the appearance that they are violating the law or the ethical standards set forth in this part. Whether particular circumstances create an appearance that the law or these standards have been violated shall be determined from the perspective of a reasonable person with knowledge of the relevant facts.

---

*GUIDELINES AND COMMENTARY*

All citizens are obliged to obey the law and to abide by regulations applicable to them. Public employees, however, have an additional burden to do so because their illegal acts take on a public dimension that goes beyond the violation itself. Laws seeking to govern their public duties are especially important. Yet even the violation of a law in the public employee's private life (drunk driving, tax evasion, drug possession) carries an additional stigma.

# II
# ARTIFICES AND SCHEMES

*STANDARD*
Public employees should not engage in artifices and schemes to exploit loopholes or ambiguities in the law in a way that undermines their spirit and purpose.

*GUIDELINES AND COMMENTARY*

When public employees seek to circumvent the spirit or purpose of laws they tend to undermine the public's confidence in government and diminish the public's commitment to civic responsibility by legitimizing self-interested evasions of public policy.

# III
# INTEGRITY OF THE PROCESS

*STANDARD*
In using procedural rules, public employees should maintain the integrity, fairness and efficiency of the process by honoring the substance and spirit of the rules and by refraining from conduct which undermines the principles of representative democracy.

Given this standard the five issues related to the integrity of the process are:

1. *Manipulation of Procedures — What Is the Improperness?*
2. *Loss of Public Respect — What Are the Consequences?*
3. *Need for Leadership — What Is the Need for Self-Restraint?*
4. *Tests of Propriety — How Do You Test Propriety?*
5. *Notice — What Is the Purpose of Giving Advance Notice?*

**GUIDELINES AND COMMENTARY**

### 1. *What Is the Improperness of Manipulating Procedures?*

The importance of technical procedures in the legislative and administrative process encourages legalistic manipulation to achieve political goals. While this is not inherently improper, there is a tendency to adopt an "ends-justifies-the-means" philosophy which can elevate process over substance and power over principle in a way that undermines fundamental assumptions of democratic government.

### 2. *What Are Consequences of Losing Public Respect?*

The public interest is not served when public employees engage in trickery or procedural extortion to achieve their ends. Generally, the public views parliamentary machinations with cynicism. Responsible public employees recognize that no specific political victory is worth damaging the delicate structure of democratic government. Legalistic maneuvering which creates unfair or anti-democratic results inevitably spawns ill will and countermeasures. Sometimes Machiavellian scheming can become so prevalent that it reduces the political process to competitive gamesmanship.

### 3. *Why Do Public Employees Need to Exercise Voluntary Self-Restraint Behavior?*

The principle that public employees have an obligation to the integrity of the democratic system to exercise voluntary self-restraint in the legal but ethically dubious use of procedures is difficult to adhere to in some political situations where expediency is more highly regarded than principle — if it's permissible, it's proper; if it works, it's justified. And, refraining from improper procedural manipulation is especially difficult in legislative contexts where opponents use such tactics and where there are important immediate rewards for winning. It is, therefore, the obligation of leaders to set a good example.

### 4. *How Do You Test Propriety?*

There is no single litmus test to know exactly when the use of a procedural maneuver crosses the line of propriety. Still, whether something is a clever but legitimate tactic or a sleazy, unfair ploy must depend on more than the perspective of winners and losers. A valuable test is: would it be good for the system if everyone used the rules in this way? A pervasive factor in evaluating the propriety of the use of rules is the appearance of fairness. An alternative approach is found in the Ethics Manual for Members and Employees of the House of Representatives (construing Clause 2 of the Code of Official Conduct, House rule XLIII) which states that it is wrong for public employees to do indirectly what they cannot do directly. If the use of procedures creates a substantive result that clearly could not have been achieved without the technical tactic, it is likely to be regarded as improper.

### 5. *What is the Purpose of Giving Advance Notice Before a Procedure?*

If the procedure does not provide adequate notice or opportunity to opponents, it often will be regarded by many as improper. For example, it is improper to suspend the rules or force a vote in a way that violates customary practices and expectations of fair notice and, therefore, prevents legitimate opposition from having its say.

## IV
## CIVIL DISOBEDIENCE

### STANDARD
In rare cases, a public employee may exercise the prerogative of conscientious objection by disobeying the law. In such cases, the illegal behavior should be open and the official should be willing to bear the appropriate legal and political consequences.

### GUIDELINES AND COMMENTARY

There is a long and revered history in this country of civil disobedience — the open and public refusal to abide by a law as a means of protest and as an impetus to change the law.

Public employees should safeguard public confidence in the integrity of government by being honest, fair, caring and respectful and by avoiding conduct creating the appearance of impropriety or which is otherwise unbefitting a public official.

# PRINCIPLE 5:
# Show Respectability and Fitness for Office

The following standards will be discussed in this section:

## I. SUITABILITY FOR PUBLIC OFFICE

### A. Honesty

### B. Integrity

### C. Private Personal Conduct

## II. ENSURING PUBLIC RESPECT

### A. What Are the Dangers of Impropriety?

### B. What Is the Importance of Avoiding Appearances of Impropriety?

# I
# SUITABILITY FOR PUBLIC OFFICE

*STANDARD*
Public employees should conduct their professional and personal lives so as to reveal character traits, attitudes, and judgments that are worthy of honor and respect and demonstrate suitability for public office.

---

**OGE RULE:**

**Section 2635.902(s)** The prohibition against employment of an individual who habitually uses intoxicating beverages to excess (5 U.S.C. 7352).

---

*GUIDELINES AND COMMENTARY*

### *What Is the Importance of Having Positive Attitudes?*

In a democracy, positive attitudes about government and the people who exercise its powers are essential to participatory citizenship. Since public employees are representatives of government, even unofficial conduct often has significant symbolic value that bears upon the public's pride, trust and confidence in government. Any conduct which damages public confidence injures the political system.

### *Why Do Public Employees Need to Be Held to High Standards of Probity?*

Public employees should be held to high standards of personal probity. Acts which demean or discredit government or demonstrate defects in their character and judgment are improper.

# I(A)
# Honesty

*STANDARD*
Public employees should be scrupulously honest, avoiding any form of lying, deception, deviousness, hypocrisy and cheating in their professional and personal lives.

---

## OGE RULES:

**2635.101(b)(12)** Employees shall satisfy in good faith their obligations as citizens, including all just financial obligations, especially those—such as Federal, State, or local taxes—that are imposed by law.

**Section 2635.809 Just financial obligations**.

Employees shall satisfy in good faith their obligations as citizens, including all just financial obligations, especially those such as Federal, State, or local taxes that are imposed by law. For purposes of this section, a just financial obligation

---

includes any financial obligation acknowledged by the employee or reduced to judgment by a court. In good faith means an honest intention to fulfill any just financial obligation in a timely manner. In the event of a dispute between an employee and an alleged creditor, this section does not require an agency to determine the validity or amount of the disputed debt or to collect a debt on the alleged creditor's behalf.

Given the standard, two issues dealing with honesty are:

1. *Dishonesty — What Are the Consequences?*
2. *Deception — What Is Its Relation to Honesty?*

**GUIDELINES AND COMMENTARY**

### 1. *What Are the Consequences of Dishonesty?*

Dishonesty by a public employee is wrong in itself but it also violates the principle of public service ethics by seriously undermining the credibility of government. A public employee who is dishonest in any significant way, even in private life, does not inspire trust and confidence in government.

### 2. *How Is Deception Related to Honesty?*

Technical or literal truthfulness is not all that is required; honesty precludes any deliberate deception including the raising of false inferences.

# I(B)
# Integrity

**STANDARD**

A public employee should reflect personal integrity in all matters, placing principle over expediency and demonstrating courage of convictions.

**GUIDELINES AND COMMENTARY**

Although it is necessary and proper for elected officials to represent the views of their constituencies, it also is necessary that they have pronounced and strong personal convictions-things they stand for. A public employee should offer principled leadership, be a compass rather than a weather vane.

# I(C)
# Private Personal Conduct

*STANDARD*
Public employees should avoid engaging in any conduct which is likely to bring discredit on themselves and the governmental bodies in which they serve.

Given this standard, three issues dealing with private personal conduct are:

1. *Professional and Private Behavior —What are the Costs of Impropriety?*
2. *Public Trust as a Matter of Perception —What is the Public Employee's Role?*
3. *Private Morality — What is Considered Inappropriate?*
    i) *Illegal and Dishonest Conduct*
    ii) *Lawful Conduct Raising Moral Issues*
    iii) *Role of the Press*

*GUIDELINES AND COMMENTARY*

1. *What Are the Costs of Impropriety in Professional and Private Behavior?*

Although there has been much discussion in recent years about a new intrusiveness of the press into the private lives of politicians, there is little doubt that virtually any behavior that would raise the moral eyebrows of a significant portion of the citizenry is subject to public disclosure in the press. Thus, public employees who choose to engage in morally challengeable conduct should do so knowing they risk exposure and personal and institutional embarrassment.

## 2. *What Is the Role of Perception When Dealing With the Issue of Public Trust?*

Since public trust is a matter of perception, and since the disclosure of dubious conduct increases cynicism about the kind of people serving government, the public employee has an extra burden to avoid such conduct.

## 3. *What Are the Issues Concerning Private Morality?*

An especially troublesome group of behaviors concern activities — drug or alcohol abuse, adultery, exploitative or promiscuous relationships, sex with minors or prostitutes, and gambling — raising issues about private morality. Whether or not these behaviors are morally "wrong," many claim they represent lifestyle choices which are not relevant to public service ethics. Other issues related to private morality conduct are:

> (i) *Illegal and Dishonest Conduct*
> (ii) *Lawful Conduct Raising Moral Issues*
> (iii) *Role of the Press*

### (i) *Illegal and Dishonest Conduct*

Activities which are illegal (e.g., drunk driving, hiring prostitutes) are clearly wrong because they violate the lawfulness mandate of public service ethics. And, private conduct revealing hypocrisy (e.g., a public official who claims to be anti-abortion recently paid for one for a girlfriend) shows a lack of integrity. The most serious questions pitting personal privacy against public duty arise when the conduct is neither illegal nor hypocritical.

### (ii) *Lawful Conduct Raising Moral Issues*

Many believe that lawful private acts which do not bear in any direct way on the responsibilities of public office are within a zone of personal privacy that should be insulated from public scrutiny or criticism. Under this theory, adultery, homosexuality and similar private behaviors should almost never be appropriate concerns of the press or public. The trend, however, is clearly against this view. Based on the argument that all personal behavior which reveals judgment and character is, by that fact alone, relevant to the public's right to know about the character of its public employees.

### (iii) *Role of the Press*

As a practical matter, the press tends to determine the pertinence of private conduct, and whether it raises issues of fitness to serve or appearances of impropriety. If morally controversial actions are reported, the public exposure tends to diminish public respect. This puts public employees who might otherwise choose to engage in some of these activities in a difficult position. They could insist righteously that it is not the public's business. But they must realize that if journalists disagree, the matter still will be treated as an impropriety and it will be made public. Thus, the individual must decide whether it is worth the personal and political risk, bearing in mind that exposure may undermine public trust in both the politician and the institution.

# II
# ENSURING PUBLIC RESPECT

*STANDARD*

In treating their office as a public trust, public servants should act so as to ensure the reality and perception that government is conducted according to the highest principles of democracy with honesty, integrity and a concern for justice and is, therefore, worthy of respect, trust and support.

---

### OGE RULES:

**Subpart A General Provisions**

**Section 2635.101 Basic obligation of public service.**

**Section 2635.101(a)** Public service is a public trust. Each employee has a responsibility to the United States Government and its citizens to place loyalty to the Constitution, laws and ethical principles above private gain. To ensure that every citizen can have complete confidence in the integrity of the Federal Government, each employee shall respect and adhere to the principles of ethical conduct set forth in this section, as

---

> well as the implementing standards contained in this part and in supplemental agency regulations.
>
> **2635.101(b) General principles**. The following general principles apply to every employee and may form the basis for the standards contained in this part. Where a situation is not covered by the standards set forth in this part, employees shall apply the principles set forth in this section in determining whether their conduct is proper.
>
> **2635.101(b)(1)** Public service is a public trust, requiring employees to place loyalty to the Constitution, the laws and ethical principles above private gain.
>
> **2635.101(b)(7)** Employees shall not use public office for private gain.

An essential condition of representative democratic government is public respect for the processes and people that make up the government. This requires faith and confidence in the commitment of government servants to use delegated public power only for the common good.

A. *Dangers of Impropriety — What Are They?*
B. *Avoiding Appearances of Impropriety — What Is the Importance?*

## II(A)
## What Are the Dangers of Impropriety?

*STANDARD*
Public servants should maintain public trust in government by avoiding acts which place personal or private interests above pursuit of the public interest.

*GUIDELINES AND COMMENTARY*

Official acts by public servants which reflect dishonesty, bias, insensitivity, unaccountability lawlessness, greed or selfishness are not only wrong in themselves, they are also wrong because they violate the trust inherent in public office and thereby undermine public confidence and respect for government. Public servants should maintain public trust in government by avoiding acts which place personal or private interests above pursuit of the public interest. While avoiding impropriety is essential, *appearances* of impropriety are equally important to address.

# II(B)
# What Is the Importance of Avoiding Appearances of Impropriety?

*STANDARD*

Public servants should avoid conduct which tends to undermine public trust by creating in the minds of reasonable impartial observers the perception that government office has been used improperly.

Since perceptions can alter a person's concept of trust, public servants (especially because they serve the public interest) have a special responsibility to avoid conduct which may generate cynical attitudes and suspicions about government and the people who administer it. If the appearance of improper conduct is displayed, it may destroy public trust even if the conduct does not actually misuse public office.

Under the standard of avoiding improprieties, four expectations are categorized in terms of:

1. *The Reasonable Person Test*
2. *Responsibility to Act*
3. *Avoiding Bad Decisions*
4. *Accountability*

*GUIDELINES AND COMMENTARY*

1. *Reasonable Person Test*

The standard to determine whether something is improper should not be set by the most suspicious and cynical members of society, but by reasonable persons with no predisposition to assume bad faith or corrupt motives.

2. *Responsibility to Act*

It is not always right to avoid an act simply because it will look wrong.

The ethical obligation to avoid the appearance of impropriety should not be used as an excuse for inaction or bureaucratic intransigence. Excess timidity in the face of possible criticism is no more justifiable than callous disregard for improper appearances. In some cases, public servants should be willing to confront criticisms and endure unfair denunciations, choosing to explain and justify their behavior rather than alter their conduct to suit the cynical perceptions of a misinformed press or public.

### 3. *Avoiding Bad Decisions*

A balance must be found between the need to preserve public confidence and the responsibility to make sound decisions on the merits. The requirement that public servants avoid even the appearance of impropriety can undermine the public interest and cause bad decisions. For example, it may force government decision makers to discriminate against friends or political supporters just because it may look bad to the public. Yet if a friend or political supporter is clearly the best qualified person available to perform a needed public task, it is unfair and unwise to automatically disqualify them.

### 4. *Accountability*

If a public servant conscientiously decides to override the appearance of impropriety test, it is important to reduce the harm to public trust by taking steps to assure that all facts relevant to the choice are made public and that the process of decision making is open and can withstand close scrutiny.

## More resources from the Josephson Institute of Ethics

The Josephson Institute of Ethics is active in all aspects of ethics education, from youth, through its CHARACTER COUNTS! initiative, to adults, through its *Ethics and Effectiveness in the Workplace* training seminars and consulting services. The Institute has also partnered with leaders in adult ethics education, from the Society for Human Resource Management to the Ethics Officer Association and the Better Business Bureau.

## Good Ideas for Creating a More Ethical and Effective Workplace

There are many things companies can do to boost ethics and morale. This book shares several innovative ideas used around the country, from hiring and firing to compensation and communication. With an extensive bonus section on writing an effective corporate ethics code.

(6" x 9", *softcover*, 124 pages)
**Item #50-1080**
**$13.99**

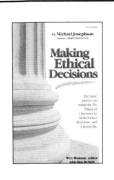

## Making Ethical Decisions

Moral questions can be knotty. This comprehensive primer examines the hows and whys of making choices that withstand ethical scrutiny. With realistic examples and a step-by-step decision-making model, this easy-to-read booklet is ideal for the individual reader — or as a training guide for any organization that wishes to help its employees find the way through difficult issues to successful choices.

(5.5" x 8.5", *softcover*, 33 pages)
**Item #50-0450**
**$7.95**

## Commentaries by Michael Josephson

Every day, listeners around the world tune in to hear Michael Josephson's take on the issues that define our days and lives. From business and world affairs to sports and parenting, Mr. Josephson offers the unique perspective of one of the country's best-known ethicists and most innovative teachers. Now his favorite commentaries — featuring the humor, compassion and tough talk he is renowned for — are available in these hardcover gift volumes and in a two-CD set.

(Books are 5" x 7", *hardcover with dust jacket*)

| | | |
|---|---|---|
| *You Don't Have to Be Sick to Get Better!* | **Item #50-5000** | **$20.00** |
| *The Best Is Yet to Come* | **Item #50-5010** | **$20.00** |
| Both books | **Item #50-5020sp** | **$35.00** |
| *Making Your Character Count* double CD | **Item #05-1190** | **$20.00** |

Order by calling (800) 711-2670 or online at: www.charactercounts.org

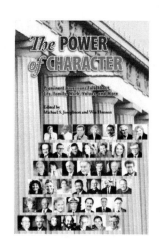
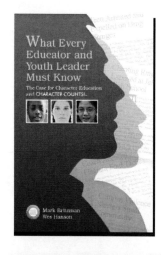